the SUPER ^simple guide to BREEDING

freshwater fishes

Laura Muha

T.F.H. Publications, Inc.

T.F.H. Publications, Inc.
One TFH Plaza
Third and Union Avenues
Neptune City, NJ 07753

*This book has been published with the intent to provide accurate and authoritative information in regard to the subject
matter within. While every precaution has been taken in preparation of this book, the author and publisher expressly disclaim responsibility for any errors, omissions, or adverse effects arising from the use or application of the information contained herein. The techniques and suggestions are used at the reader's discretion and are not to be considered a substitute for veterinary care. If you suspect a medical problem consult your veterinarian.*

Library of Congress Cataloging-in-Publication Data
Muha, Laura.
The super simple guide to breeding freshwater fishes / Laura Muha.
p. cm.
Includes index.
ISBN 0-7938-3457-0 (alk. paper)
1. Aquarium fishes-Breeding. 2. Freshwater fishes-Breeding. I. Title.
SF457.9.M84 2005
639.34--dc22
2004031012

Dedicated to the care and well-being of companion animals for over 50 years.
www.tfhpublications.com

Contents

Dedication

This book is dedicated to my nephew, Benjamin Pace Muha, who has been leaving noseprints on my fish tanks since the day he was tall enough to reach them.

Part One

"Edna! So nice of you to drop by!
Have you met our three thousand children?"

Acknowledgments

The author wishes to express appreciation to the following individuals and associations for their assistance during the research and preparation of this book: Jay Hecker and David Boozer of the Florida Fish Farmers Association; Rit Forcier of The American Livebearer Association; Russ Taylor of the Goldfish Society of America; Dr. Craig A. Watson of the Department of Fisheries and Aquatic Sciences, the University of Florida; Dr. Lee Alan Dugatkin, associate professor of biology, the University of Louisville; Dr. Albert J. Klee, aquatic historian and co-founder of the American Killifish Association; Rosario LaCorte, breeder and author, North Jersey Aquarium Society; the staff of Tropiquarium, Ocean, N.J.; the American Pet Products Manufacturers Association; and Dr. George

M. Muha, professor emeritus of chemistry, Rutgers University (thanks, Dad!).

Special thanks go to Matt Conley and Joe Graffagnino, who have been unfailingly generous with their time and expertise; and, of course, to Beryl C. Taylor, VMD, who not only provided invaluable advice during the preparation of this manuscript, but who also patiently totes buckets during water changes, puts up with an ever-growing assortment of fish tanks, and never forgets to feed the pleco.

Why Breed Aquarium Fish?

No one knows exactly when the first fish were bred in captivity, but it's safe to say the practice goes back thousands of years. Hieroglyphics on the walls of Egyptian tombs built around 2500 B.C. depict tilapia and mormyrids, fish the Egyptians are believed to have cultivated not just for food but for decoration and enjoyment.

Aquariums of all types have been used to house and breed fishes for many years.

The modern-day approach to

breeding ornamental fish, with its emphasis on form and color, has its roots in China, where more than a thousand years ago, fishkeepers began selectively mating goldfish to produce specimens that were red, black, and gold instead of the drab greenish-brown of their wild cousins. The Japanese got into the act in the 1500s, refining the art and science of selective breeding even further, and by the 1700s, the practice had spread to Europe.

Paradise Fish were one of the first tropical fishes to be bred by hobbyists in North America.

In North America, a few species of hardy coldwater fish, including the Two-spined Stickleback and the Bullhead Catfish, were being bred in aquariums by the 1860s; a decade later, the paradise fish joined their ranks, becoming one of the first tropical species to do so. But it wasn't until the advent of effective filtration and temperature controls in the 1930s, coupled with a better understanding of water chemistry, that breeding fish became something more than a handful of people could do.

Today, the majority of fish for sale in North American pet shops are bred at commercial fish farms in Florida and Southeast Asia. But that doesn't mean amateur breeders don't play a vital role in the hobby. Every year, they trade and sell thousands of fish among themselves–including rare species of fish that are almost never seen in pet shops. Some of those species, such as the Mexican Goodeid *(Skiffia francesae)*, are no longer found in the wild and would be virtually extinct if amateurs weren't breeding them in captivity. In addition, there are many things ichthyologists (a fancy word for scientists who study fish) don't know about the reproductive strategies of their subjects. So amateur breeders who keep careful data about what goes on in their tanks have the opportunity to contribute to a larger body of scientific knowledge–while getting to say they're a part of a tradition that dates back thousands of years!

Why Breed Fish?

Few fishkeepers forget the thrill they felt the first time they found fry in one of their tanks. Often, the sighting was unexpected–perhaps they purchased a female livebearer without realizing she was pregnant, or had no idea their fish had spawned until they caught sight of a tiny fry zigzagging among the big guys at feeding time.

The excitement of such an accidental encounter is often enough to jump start a hobbyist's interest in breeding; it may even be the reason you bought this book. But a few accidental spawns are one thing; breeding fish successfully over the long term is another. The latter is the result of careful planning, realistic goals, hard work, and attention to detail. A good place to begin a discussion of this is by examining some of the reasons you might want to breed fish.

Four Keys to Becoming a Successful Breeder

- Start with healthy, compatible fish of reproductive age.
- Feed them well.
- Provide the right environment— especially water chemistry.
- Provide them with the appropriate environmental triggers, if any.

Breeding for Profit

This is one of the motives most often cited by beginning breeders. After all, fishkeeping can be an expensive hobby, and what better way to underwrite it than by producing cute little fish in your very own tank and selling them for a profit–or so the reasoning goes. The reality is that while it's not impossible to make money breeding fish, it's difficult. Many pet shops won't take fry from hobbyists, and the hassle and expense associated with selling directly to other aquarists often outweigh the financial benefits. For now, suffice it to say that if your chief motivation for breeding fish is to make a profit, you should, at the very least, do some serious market research first.

Terms to Know

Species: A group of organisms that share a unique set of genetically determined characteristics, such as physical form. Members of a species can breed with one another but not other species, unless the two are very closely related.

Crossbreeding: This is breeding that occurs across species lines. Although this rarely occurs in the wild, it is common in captivity, where fish don't always have the option of mating with a member of their own species they sometimes mate with a member of another.

Hybrid: The crossbred offspring of two species. Hybrids typically have some traits of both parents, and are often—but not always—sterile.

Morph, strain, or variety: An organism that differs from other members of its species in minor ways, such as color or body shape. In nature, morphs develop naturally over the course of many generations. In captivity, the timetable can be significantly condensed by aquarists who set out to create new patterns and fin shapes by selectively mating fish.

But that's not to say there aren't plenty of rewards inherent in breeding fish—even if getting rich isn't one of them. What follows are just a few.

Breeding for Educational Purposes

Fish exhibit some of their most interesting behavior when they're spawning, and breeding them in aquaria will give you a front-row seat—something that would be impossible in the wild. And if you have kids, what better way to instill in them respect for the natural world and at the same time expose them to something that has the potential to become a lifelong interest?

Breeding Because It's Challenging

Many hobbyists consider breeding to be one of the most significant challenges in fishkeeping, and a great way to test their skills as aquarists. A closed environment like an aquarium is an unnatural setting for a fish, so it's incredibly satisfying to know you created conditions so close to Mother Nature's that your fish were induced to spawn. Plus, there are many levels of skill to develop as a breeder; once you get the hang of some of the easier-to-spawn species, there are dozens of harder species you can try—including some that have never before been bred in aquariums.

Breeding for Conservation

There are more than 185 million freshwater fish swimming around home aquariums in the United States, and they all have to come from somewhere. While the majority of fish on the market are bred in captivity, millions of dollars' worth of some popular species— including Clown Loaches, Harlequin Rasboras, and Arowanas—are still being captured in the wild and sold to the pet trade every year, a practice that is putting a large dent in their native populations. Habitat destruction has contributed to dwindling numbers of other wild populations of freshwater fish, including Cherry Barbs, certain killifish, and Bala Sharks. By breeding fish in captivity, hobbyists can help dry up the market for wild-caught fish, and preserve species that would otherwise be at risk of extinction.

Breeding as a Social Activity

Breeding fish doesn't have to be a solitary hobby. Many aquarium clubs sponsor breeding programs in which aquarists earn points (and sometimes awards) for the number and types of fish they breed, moving through a series of ranks, from novice to grand master breeder. It's a great opportunity to make friends and share ideas and information, learning even more about your hobby as you do.

The Biology of Breeding Fish

The survival of any species depends on two things: The ability of its members to produce offspring, and the ability of those offspring to continue the cycle by having progeny of their own.

Individuals who are weak or ill adapted to the rigors of their environment–whether it is in a desert pool in the American

The good genetics of these live-bearers is apparent by several generations living together in one tank.

Southwest or in one of the Rift Lakes in Africa–often perish before reaching maturity. Those who are strong and healthy enough to find food, escape predators, and resist disease will likely survive and eventually reproduce, passing on these traits to their offspring via their genetic code.

As a result, each species gradually evolves over many thousands of years, fine-tuning the physical and behavioral characteristics that help it to succeed in its environment and weeding out those that do not.

Scientifically Speaking

Most fish have a scientific name and a common name. Experienced aquarists use the former because the common name—while easier to pronounce and remember—tends to vary from place to place, causing confusion. For example, the Pearl Gourami is also called the Lace Gourami, the Diamond Gourami, the Platinum Gourami, the Leeri Gourami, and the Mosaic Gourami. However, it has only one scientific name, *Trichogaster leeri*, which is the same no matter what language you speak. *Trichogaster* refers to the genus, or taxonomic group, to which the species belongs, and *leeri* identifies the species itself. Occasionally, fish have more than one scientific name, reflecting disagreement among scientists about how to classify them.

If you want to breed fish, it's important to understand this complex interplay between fishes and their surroundings, as well as the reproductive strategies that have evolved in response to them. That way, when problems come up–as they inevitably will–you will be able to think them through and come up with an array of possible solutions, something that will go a long way toward ensuring the success of your breeding program.

Methods of Reproduction

Just about all freshwater aquarium fish reproduce sexually–that is, by combining egg and sperm–but the process by which that occurs, and the rearing of fry that follows, will vary widely from one species to another. Some fish are monogamous (at least during the course of a single breeding cycle), while others will spawn with numerous partners. Some guard their eggs or young, while others are seemingly oblivious to them–or even go so far as to eat them. Generally speaking, though, fish employ one of two reproductive strategies: They either lay eggs or give birth to live fry.

Livebearers

This is the reproductive strategy most comparable to human reproduction. Female livebearers produce eggs, which the male fertilizes by touching his gonopodium to her vent or releasing sperm in it's vicinity. At the end of a gestational period (which can vary in length according to light and water temperature), the female delivers fully-developed fry.

There are a few key differences between human reproduction and that of livebearers, however. For one thing, female livebearers are capable of having a lot more babies at once–often 100 or more, depending on species and the size of the mother. And unlike their human counterparts, many female livebearers can store sperm internally; after giving birth to one batch of fry, they use the stored sperm to fertilize another batch of eggs. In fact, it's not uncommon for a female to give birth to several batches of fry from a single insemination over a period of several months. That's one of the reasons female livebearers, such as guppies or platys, sometimes

Swordtails are a good choice for the beginning breeder.

Some of the best-known live-bearers are platys, swordtails, guppies, mollies, and goodeids.

have what appears to be a virgin birth, delivering fry in tanks where there was no male present to have fathered them.

Once the fry are born, their mother's job is done; she not only does not care for the babies, but she does not seem to recognize them as her offspring and may even try to eat them.

Egg Layers

This is by far the most common means of reproduction among fish. Unlike their livebearing counterparts, egg-laying fish do not fertilize or incubate their young internally. Rather, they release eggs and sperm into the water, and when the two come into contact with one another, fertilization takes place. Within the broad category of egg layers, however, fish employ a wide range of different reproductive strategies: Some scatter their eggs; some build nests for them; some deposit them on rocks, wood, or plants; some brood them in their mouths; and a few even bury them.

Egg Scatterers

Egg-scattering fish practice what could be thought of as the aquatic version of free love. They spawn in mid-water, with the females releasing eggs and the males simultaneously releasing a cloud of sperm–a process that can be so fast that it occurs in less than a second as the fish swim past one another. The breeding pair then

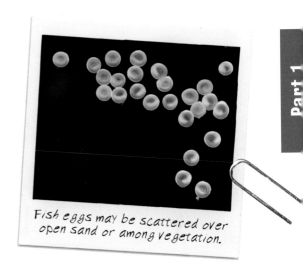

Fish eggs may be scattered over open sand or among vegetation.

goes on their separate ways, leaving their eggs to drift down through the water column and land where they may. Those that land in a protected site, such as a rock crevice, may hatch, while those that land in the open are often eaten by other fish, including their own parents. To compensate for this and to ensure that some of their eggs go on to hatch and the fry grow to adulthood, fish that spawn using this strategy tend to produce large numbers of eggs, typically numbering in the hundreds or even thousands. Zebra Danios, Neon Tetras, and Bala Sharks are examples of egg-scattering fish.

Egg Depositors

Rather than spawn wherever they happen to be when the urge hits, egg depositors deliberately seek out a site in (or on) which to spawn. Some are known as *plant choosers* because they spawn in clumps of vegetation; others are called *substrate choosers* because they pick a site, such as a piece of wood or a rock, on which to lay

Here, Pink Convict cichlids deposit a batch of eggs in a submerged flowerpot.

their eggs. In the home aquarium, such fish sometimes consider just about anything to be "substrate," even spawning on the heater or the sides of the tank.

Males of plant-spawning species typically chase or lure the female into a clump of vegetation or a spawning mop; once there, she releases her eggs either en masse or a few at a time, and he simultaneously releases sperm to fertilize them. Substrate choosers frequently clean off their designated spawning site together beforehand.

Plant-spawning parents, such as rainbowfish and some species of killifish, are similar to egg scatterers in that they typically do not guard their eggs. Substrate spawners, however, sometimes do. Discus and angelfish are examples of substrate-choosing fish that guard their eggs.

Mouthbrooders

As their name indicates, mouthbrooders incubate their eggs and/or fry in their mouths to keep them safe from predators—a reproductive strategy that makes them one of the most interesting fish to breed.

Typically, the process begins with the female depositing her eggs on a flat surface, such as a rock, where the male fertilizes them; one parent then gathers them in his or her mouth and incubates them.

Mouthbrooding is a very popular spawning technique used by many species of cichlids.

There are a couple of variations on this: In a few species of mouthbrooders, the female releases the eggs and picks them up immediately; the male then fertilizes them by releasing sperm into her mouth. And a few species of South American cichlids allow their eggs to hatch in a nest and then gather the fry in their mouths to protect them from predators as they grow—a technique known as *delayed mouthbrooding*.

Usually, the female is the one who does the mouthbrooding; however, there are some species in which that task is relegated to the male and even a few in which both parents share in it equally. This strategy is known as *biparental mouthbrooding*.

Cichlids are among the best-known examples of mouthbrooders, although there are other species that also practice this reproductive strategy, such as some species of bettas.

Nest Builders
Like birds, some fish build nests in which to lay and incubate their

eggs. In most cases, either the mother or father remains with them to protect them until they hatch and the fry become free swimming. There are two different types of nesting strategies commonly employed by fish—bubble nesting and pit nesting.

Bubble nesters construct elaborate floating nests of saliva bubbles, and in some cases, snippets of vegetation. The breeding pair spawns directly under it, and the fertilized eggs either float into the nest or are picked up by the male and spit into it. The male then guards the nest until the fry hatch and become free swimming. Bettas and gouramis are among the best-known bubble-nest builders.

Pit nesters dig holes in the substrate in which to lay their eggs. The female releases them into the nest, and the male fertilizes them there. At least one of the parents then stands guard over the eggs, fanning fresh water over them with their fins, until the fry hatch and become free swimming. Many catfishes and some cichlids build pit nests in which to spawn.

Other Strategies

Some fish will only spawn in enclosed spaces such as caves or shells. A few fish even bury their eggs to protect them. Some killifish, for instance, deposit their eggs in the mud, then die when the water dries up. The eggs remain

This female *Neolamprologus ocellatus* has moved her fry to a shallow pit.

dormant in the substrate, hatching the following year, when the rainy season restores their habitat.

The Breeder's Role

Now that you know something about the reproductive strategies of fish, let's talk about the role that you, the aquarist, plays in getting them to reproduce. The most important thing to remember in this regard is that *you* don't really breed your fish. They breed themselves, as long as you provide them with three things: a compatible mate of reproductive age, the right environment, and the diet they need to stay healthy. Let's consider these factors separately.

The Right Mate

Fish reproduce sexually, so obviously you'll need at least one male and one female of a given species in order for them to spawn. What's not always so obvious, however, is which is which.

Every species, fish included, have what are known as *primary sex characteristics*–that is, body structures specific to reproduction, such as ovaries and testicles. The problem is that the only way to see them is to dissect the fish.

That means that aquarists must rely on *secondary sex characteristics*–

Many suckermouth catfishes use improvised caves as spawning sites.

gender-linked physical traits other than the reproductive organs–to distinguish between male and female fish. In humans, secondary sex characteristics include breasts in women and facial hair in men. In fish, secondary sex characteristics can include size, body shape, coloration, markings, fin shape, and/or behavior.

Some fish are *dimorphic,* meaning that it's easy to tell males and females apart by their secondary sex characteristics. Male Pearl Gouramis have robin's-red breasts and long, pointed dorsal fins, while females have shorter, more rounded dorsal fins and silvery breasts. Male bristlenose catfishes have much larger bristles than females. And males and females of many species of livebearers can be distinguished by differences in their anal fins: While those of females (and juveniles) are fan shaped, those of males thicken and fuse as they mature to form what is known as a gonopodium–a tube-like copulatory organ used for internal fertilization of the female.

Unfortunately, not all fish display such obvious sex-linked characteristics. In some species, males and females resemble one another so closely that even the most skilled aquarists can't always tell them apart. Neon Tetras, for example, are extremely difficult to sex, although some aquarists say they are able to tell the difference by examining the fish in profile; the females have deeper, more rounded bellies than the males, who have a straighter line from jaw to tail. However, that's not a perfect predictor, since a well-fed male and an undernourished female could easily be confused with one another.

In other words, a certain percentage of fish will fail to spawn because the aquarist has unwittingly paired two males or two females. Sometimes, the drive to reproduce is so strong that the fish court one another anyway, and in the case of two females, may even lay eggs. The poor aquarist is then left scratching his or her head, wondering why no fry resulted from what appeared to be such a vigorous courtship.

The Venting Technique

Males and females of some difficult-to-sex species, including many American cichlids, can be distinguished from one another by a process known as *venting*. It involves removing the fish from the water and turning it upside down to examine the shape of its genital pore, a small pimple-like structure located between the anus and the tail. In females, the genital pore is typically shorter and wider than it is in males. However, the differences can be quite subtle and difficult to determine without repeatedly comparing the fish to one another. Since being removed from the water is stressful for the fish, the process must be carried out quickly and efficiently, and is usually best left to experienced breeders.

An easier way to solve the problem of difficult-to-sex fish is by buying a group of at least a half dozen juveniles, ensuring a better-than-90-percent chance of having a mix of both males and females. You can then raise the fish together, allowing them to pair off naturally. It is usually evident when they have done so, particularly in fish such as cichlids that form strong pair bonds, because the male and female stake out a territory together and drive other fish away from it.

The other thing to remember when selecting compatible breeding pairs is that the reproductive life of a fish, like that of a human, has a beginning and an end. Some loaches, for example, appear to be full grown when they're around a year old, but will rarely spawn

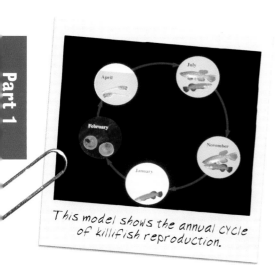

This model shows the annual cycle of killifish reproduction.

before they're two or three. And most bettas stop reproducing by the time they're about 14 months old—important to know, since many are nearly a year old by the time they reach a pet shop.

In addition, fish that are badly malnourished or have been kept for an extended period in poor-quality water. sometimes suffer physical damage that affects their ability to breed. Even when conditions improve, the damage may be irreversible, leaving them unable to reproduce.

Serious breeders often buy their breeding stock from pet shops. This way they can see the juvenile fishes before comitting to them. That enables the breeder to hand select the best stock and raise them to maturity—something that not only enables them to know exactly how old the fish are, but to control the conditions under which they grow and mature.

The Right Environment

Let's examine how a fish's environment affects the likelihood that it will spawn. There are three elements to consider:
• Physical setup
• Water quality
• Breeding triggers

Some fish aren't fussy about any of the above. Many livebearers, for instance, will breed just about anywhere, anytime. But other fish are so finicky that if they're placed in a tank that makes them feel cramped or in water that doesn't have just the right pH, they'll refuse to spawn. Some species also require a little extra nudge from Mother Nature in the form of an environmental change–a sudden decrease or increase in temperature, for instance–to jump start the breeding cycle. Let's examine these elements individually.

Physical Setup

Fish, like all living creatures, are products of their environment. Over thousands of years, they have evolved physically and behaviorally to meet the demands of their surroundings. Of necessity, they've adapted their reproductive strategies to those surroundings as well. It wouldn't do any good to be a plant spawner, after all, if home were the rocky depths of Africa's Lake Tanganyika.

Soon, this female platy will be looking for a secure place to release her babies.

The general criteria for spawning tanks will be discussed at greater length in the equipment section of the next chapter, and specific setups for individual fish will be covered in the second half of the book. For now, just keep in mind that in order to spawn fish successfully, you'll need to provide your fish with the elements that are key to the breeding process in their native habitat, whether that means thickets of plants (or their artificial equivalent), flat rocks on which to lay their eggs, substrate in which to dig nests, or caves in which to spawn.

Water Quality

Not all water is chemically equal. If you sent samples of tap water from New York City; Des Moines, Iowa; and Pasadena, California to a lab for analysis, the results would be very different. That's because water contains more than just hydrogen and oxygen molecules. It can also contain varying amounts of heavy metals, dissolved minerals, gases, nitrogen compounds, and chemicals such as chlorine–not to mention organic and inorganic pollutants.

The point isn't to turn this chapter into a lesson in Water Quality 101; if you've been keeping fish long enough to consider breeding them, you're already aware of the very important role that good water quality plays in the health and well being of your fish. But it is worth looking at the impact some properties of water can have on the breeding process, because fish that usually aren't fussy about the water you keep them in can get downright finicky when it comes to spawning. In addition, the presence of certain compounds in the water can be damaging to the eggs or fry.

Water quality will play a crucial role in the success of breeding difficult species such as many killifishes.

Here are some of the properties of water that can affect your success as a breeder:

Nitrogen compounds–When organic materials such as fish waste and uneaten food break down in aquarium water, they produce nitrogen-based compounds such as ammonia, nitrites, and nitrates. If you've been keeping fish for even a short time, you probably already know that the presence of even small amounts of ammonia and nitrites in the water is stressful to them. What you may not know is that eggs and fry are even more sensitive than adult fish and may be stunted or die if levels are even a little bit elevated. It's important to make sure there are no traces of ammonia or nitrites in breeding or rearing tanks, and to make sure nitrates stay within acceptable limits. The best way to reduce nitrates is to do a water change. The best way to prevent ammonia and nitrites is to use a mature filter in the tanks, do regular water changes, and test the water frequently.

pH–This is a measure of the acidity or alkalinity of water. The pH scale runs from 0 to 14, with 7.0 being considered neutral. Water with a higher pH is referred to as basic or alkaline, and water with a lower pH is referred to as acidic. Each fish species has a preferred pH range within

Young fishes are very sensitive to sudden changes in pH and high concentrations of nitrogen.

which it is most comfortable, although many can adapt to a higher or lower pH.

But just because they can live in it doesn't mean they'll breed in it. Because of the way fish have evolved in their native habitats, the pH at which they'll spawn is often somewhat lower than their "everyday" pH, and they're less likely to be flexible about it. In addition, pH can affect the male-to-female ratio of some species of fry; for instance, rainbowfish that breed in acidic water often produce more males, while alkaline water produces more females.

If you wish to breed fish that prefer a pH lower than that of your tap water, you can alter it using a variety of methods: filtering the water over peat (be sure to use aquarium-grade peat, since the peat available in garden centers may contain harmful fertilizers); bubbling carbon dioxide into the water, or using commercial compounds, such as humic acid extracts, that are available at your aquarium shop.

Fish rarely require a pH higher than their normal range in which to breed. However, if you wish to keep fish that prefer water more alkaline than that of your tap, you can increase it by adding oyster shells or rocks containing limestone to the tank, or by adding baking soda.

Hardness–This is a measure of the dissolved mineral salts, particularly calcium carbonate and magnesium carbonate, present in water. These salts, which occur naturally in the earth, dissolve when they are exposed to the water in underground springs. The quantity in the water depends on where it comes from and the treatment processes it undergoes. Water with a high proportion of dissolved minerals is called *hard*, and water with a low proportion is called *soft*.

The hardness of water is critical to breeding because it affects *osmotic pressure*–the flow of water across cell membranes. While adult fish can usually adapt to water that is harder or softer than their optimal range, their eggs and sperm often cannot. If the water is too hard, the outer membrane of the fish's eggs may toughen, hindering fertilization or preventing the eggs from hatching. And if the water is too soft, the eggs and sperm may take on so much water that they literally burst.

The hardness of the water also determines its *buffering* capacity–that is, its ability to absorb acids (such as those produced by fish waste) without a drop in pH. If the buffering capacity of your water is too low, your tank may experience pH swings that could harm your fish, eggs, and fry; adding baking soda will increase the buffering capacity, but will also raise pH. On the other hand, if your water has a high buffering capacity, you will have to go to considerable trouble to lower the pH, because the buffers will keep pushing it back up. To solve this, you can process your water through an ion exchanger that swaps magnesium carbonate and

Test Kits

Most aquarium stores sell two types of water test kits: paper strips that change color according to the pH level or the presence of nitrogen compounds, and liquid reagents that are added drop by drop to vials of tank water; the water itself turns a color if ammonia, nitrites, or nitrates are present. Test strips are easier, but liquid reagents are a bit more accurate—something to keep in mind if you want to breed very sensitive fish.

Water that is too "hard" will have a negative effect on the eggs of fishes that prefer "soft" water.

calcium carbonate for sodium (a salt that has no effect on hardness), or through a reverse osmosis unit, which removes all dissolved solids from the water by filtering it through a membrane.

There are many different ways to measure and express hardness. One common scale (which is the one used in this book) measures it in terms of dH, or *degree of hardness*, while another expresses it as GH, or *general hardness*, and a third measures it terms of ppm, or *parts per million*. All are equally valid–the one you use is likely to depend on which brand of test kit you purchase. Many also include conversion charts to help you switch from one to another.

Dissolved gases–Water absorbs atmospheric oxygen and carbon dioxide in a process called *gas exchange*, which takes place at the water's surface. Fish take in oxygen as water passes across their gill membranes, and give off carbon dioxide in return. The more agitation at the water's surface, the greater the amount of oxygen that passes into the water, and the greater the amount of carbon dioxide released. This is particularly critical in incubators and rearing tanks, since eggs and fry are even more sensitive to low oxygen levels than adult fish. For example, eggs will grow fungus if the oxygen level of the water is too low. Aerating the tanks with an airstone is a good way to facilitate gas exchange.

Temperature–While it's perhaps unfair to call temperature a property of water, it does play an important role not just in inducing spawning but also in the rate at which fry hatch. Eggs that incubate in warmer water will hatch sooner than those kept in cooler water; likewise, higher temperatures encourage fry to grow faster.

These Paradise Fish need warm temperatures in order to mate successfully.

Conductivity–Conductivity is a measure of the water's ability to carry an electrical current. It is related to hardness, in that water with many dissolved minerals is more conductive than extremely soft water. However, conductivity, which is measured in units known as *microsiemens*, also measures sodium ions, as well as some other substances that do not affect the hardness of water.

Although amateur breeders traditionally have not paid much attention to conductivity, some scientists believe it may have a larger role in spawning some species than initially thought. For instance, researchers have been able to prompt some fish in the Mormyridae family to breed simply by changing the conductivity of the water in which they were kept. And some species, such as discus, also breed more readily when the conductivity falls within a particular range. Although most species that are fussy about conductivity fall outside the scope of this book, it's something to keep in mind if you're interested in trying your hand at some of the hard-to-breed fish. Electronic conductivity meters can be ordered through companies that manufacture aquatic instruments.

Heavy metals–Tap water can also hold dissolved-metal ions such as iron, magnesium, lead, zinc, and copper. This last in particular is poisonous to fish and sometimes leaches into tap water from old copper pipes. It should go without saying that if heavy metals are present to such a degree that fish are stressed, they are unlikely to breed. Most water conditioners contain chelating agents that bind heavy metals in tap water. Alternatively, they can also be filtered out by an ion-exchange water softener.

Chlorine and/or chloramines–These chemicals are used by utility companies to purify the drinking water supply. They are toxic to fish, and must be neutralized either by aging the water for 24 hours before adding it to the tank or by using a water conditioner. Although any experienced fishkeeper already knows this, it's worth repeating, especially since both breeding fish and raising fry often require frequent, large water changes.

Water low in heavy metals is best when trying to breed sensitive fishes such as Discus.

Breeding Triggers
In the wild, there are certain environmental signals, or triggers, that tell the fish it's time to spawn. Often, these are linked to seasonal changes

that in turn set off a series of environmental changes: For instance, the arrival of the rainy season in the tropics may cause the pH, hardness, and temperature of lakes and rivers to drop and their depth to increase; they also flood their banks, creating shallows that are warmed by the sun. Vegetation flourishes, as do insects and crustaceans, all of which provide a sudden change in diet for fish. There may also be barometric changes, higher oxygen levels in the water, and increased water flow. Some or all of these changes may stimulate physical changes in fish necessary for the production of eggs and sperm.

Even in captivity, such environmental triggers may be required to get some species to breed. But because no obvious climate shifts take place in the home aquarium, breeders must come up with ways to simulate these environmental cues. Among the common triggers and ways to mimic them in captivity:

Changes in water chemistry–Most often the trigger is a drop in pH or hardness. The easiest way to simulate it is to do a water change–or a number of changes over a period of time–using water with the desired values.

Changes in depth–The trigger can be an increase, a decrease, or both. Obviously, this is simple to simulate by adding or removing tank water.

Automatic water changers have proved to be very useful in professional breeding setups.

Changes in the light cycle–The trigger is usually increased hours of daylight and is easy to simulate by adjusting the tank lights. Morning sun also triggers spawning in some fish; place their tank where it will receive natural sunlight.

Increased oxygenation–The colder, faster-moving waters typical of a rainy season in the tropics carry more oxygen than does warmer, slower water. An air pump and airstone can give the same result in a breeding tank.

Storms–Sudden, violent rainstorms trigger some fish to spawn. Some breeders actually simulate them for their fish, providing "rain" via watering cans, and lightning and thunder through flashing strobe lights and aluminum pans banged into microphones. Although many swear this works, to date no scientific studies bear this out. Rather, many scientists believe fish respond not to the visible (and audible) aspects of the storms, but to the changes in barometric pressure that accompany them–something a bit harder to simulate in the home aquarium! Instead, try setting your fish up to spawn when you know a storm is imminent. (However, if you are trying to breed a recalcitrant species and want to try simulating one, it certainly won't hurt!)

Changes in temperature–Dropping the temperature by two or three degrees overnight, then raising it again in the morning, can trigger spawning in some species. Some will also respond to a water change using water with a lower temperature than that of the tank.

Changes in diet–Mother Nature has programmed most fish to breed at times when plenty of food will be available for their fry. From an evolutionary standpoint, that makes a lot of sense: If there weren't enough food, the fry–and ultimately the species–would be at risk of dying out. So it's no surprise that a sudden influx of food or the appearance of certain types of food–usually live foods– can serve as a trigger, telling fish it's time to spawn. Diet is such an important part of the breeding process that an entire chapter will be devoted to it later in the book. For now, just keep in mind that what you feed your fish is one of the most important factors in their ability to produce healthy fry.

An increase in fresh foods will be needed to condition predatory fishes for spawning.

A Word About Hybrids

In nature, fish rarely seem to interbreed. Not only have they have been programmed to respond to the colors, patterns, and courtship behaviors of members of their own species, but their eggs tend to be more easily fertilized by same-species sperm as well. Given the opportunity, fish will almost always choose a partner of their own species.

In captivity, however, such opportunities are not always available. And the drive to reproduce is so strong that males and females of closely related species sometimes interbreed, producing hybrid offspring.

> ## Peer Pressure?
>
> When it comes to choosing a mate, some women look to their girlfriends for advice. Female fish, it turns out, may not be so different.
>
> In one experiment, researchers put a female guppy known to prefer bright orange males into a tank with two prospective mates—one bright orange, and the other more drab in color. The tank was partitioned so the fish couldn't get to each other.
>
> A second female was placed into the tank near the drab male, and the first female was allowed to observe them courting for ten minutes. Then the partitions were removed so she could choose a mate. Seventeen out of 20 times, she chose the drabber male. The researchers' conclusion was that peer influence may play a role in guppy relationships—just as it does in those of humans.

While this often occurs accidentally–the result of an aquarist innocently placing two similar species in the same tank–breeders sometimes cross species deliberately in an attempt to cash in on the public's demand for new and interesting fish. Some even add hormones to the water in an attempt to induce different species to interbreed. Blood parrots and flowerhorn cichlids–neither of which exists in the wild–are examples of man-made hybrids that have become very fashionable among some hobbyists.

While some breeders argue that such crossbreeding contributes to scientific knowledge of fish and their reproductive strategies, others believe it is arrogant and unethical for humans to think they can improve upon nature. With more than 20,000 known fish species already out there, they say, there is no need to create new ones. In addition, the exaggerated physical traits that make hybrids so unusual–and therefore popular–can also cause problems for them.

Blood Parrots, for example, sometimes have trouble eating because their mouths do not close normally, and their egg-shaped bodies make it difficult for them to swim rapidly.

Therefore, most responsible breeders suggest the following:
• Do not place species of fish that crossbreed in the same aquarium.
• If fish do accidentally crossbreed, destroy the eggs or cull the young.
• Alternatively, keep the fry for your enjoyment, but do not sell, trade, or give them to other hobbyists unless you are certain they are not to be further bred.
• Do not allow hybrid fish to breed, something that only perpetuates the cycle.
• Do not encourage crossbreeding by buying hybrids from pet shops or other hobbyists.

Looks may not be everything...

. . . but they play a big role when it comes to how female fish choose their mates.

In one experiment, researchers gave female mosquitofish the choice between a large male and a small one; the females consistently chose the larger male. And when female Sailfin Mollies were presented with a series of "dummy" males of varying body and fin size, they spent more time swimming near those who were larger or had more impressive sailfins.

Behavior also appears to play a role in mate selection. Male guppies, for instance, will often cautiously approach predatory fish to "inspect" them—but only when females are present. And female guppies consistently prefer the males who swim closest to the predator, which researchers speculate may be because it demonstrates strength and prowess—traits the females want to pass on to their offspring.

Planning Ahead

Different species of fish have different needs when it comes to spawning. Some require little more than a compatible mate, while others require huge tanks, complicated setups, and massive daily water changes–things that may necessitate a large investment of time, effort, and money on the part of their keeper. Likewise, different species of fry require different

Oscars are capable of producing thousands of fry.

tank sizes, diets, and water chemistry in order to grow and thrive; those needs can vary somewhat from one developmental stage to the next. Your success as a breeder will hinge on your ability to meet the needs of both adults and fry, so it's crucial to do a little homework before embarking on a breeding program.

Start by asking yourself the following questions:
• Which fish do I want to breed, and what's required to breed them?
• Do I have the time, money, and space to meet those requirements?
• What are the requirements of the fry produced by that species, and do I have the time, money, and space to meet those requirements?
• What will I do with the fry?

If you haven't already decided which fish you want to breed–and even if you have–you might find it useful to skip ahead for a moment to Part 2 of this book, where you'll find a discussion of the requirements for spawning many of the most popular species of fish. Then you can more realistically assess whether you have what it will take to breed them and to raise their offspring.

When considering which fish to breed, it's also worth doing a little market research by checking aquarium shops in your area to see which fish are selling and for how much. Even if you're well equipped to breed and raise a particular species, you don't want to be in the position of trying to get rid of hundreds of fry that nobody wants.

Speaking of which, you'd be surprised at how many people begin breeding fish with nothing more than a nebulous plan to sell the offspring to the local pet shop. When they show up at the shop, their first batch of fry in hand, they're dismayed to discover that the shop won't take them, and are left either cramming them back into their own tanks or frantically trying to find other ways to get rid of them. So, obvious as it should probably be, it's also important to think through the various options for marketing fry, because if you have even modest success as a breeder, you'll soon be inundated with them.

What to Do With All Those Fry!

There are many, many options for discarding extra fry from overly productive parents. Some are easier than others and what follows are the most common options used by hobbyists for getting rid of excess fry.

Selling or Trading Them to Pet Shops

It pays to call around before you start counting on this option, because as we've already noted, many pet shops don't take fry from hobbyists. And those that do are unlikely to take them until they're close to "saleable size" (translation: half to three-quarters of their average adult size), because they don't want to put in the time and effort–not to mention tank space–to raise young fish themselves. That means you'll be responsible for maintaining the fish until they reach saleable size–something that, depending on the species, may take a considerable amount of effort, resources, and space. It's also important to realize that even if a pet shop takes your fry, you're not likely to get anywhere close to the price that the store sells them for, because the store must factor in the expense of caring for them for however long it takes to sell them. The problem is that it's not only more efficient to purchase fish from a wholesaler, but it's safer because the store knows that if there's a problem with a batch of them, there's recourse. However, sometimes shops are willing to take fish that sell easily but don't ship well from amateur breeders. Some will also trade juvenile fish for store credit.

Auctioning Them Off

If you're not already a member of your local aquarium club, now's the time to join. Not only will you find experienced aquarists willing to provide advice and support for your breeding program, but you'll also find an easy outlet for your fry, since many aquarium clubs regularly auction fish bred by members. (The club usually takes a small portion of the proceeds, and the rest goes to the breeder.) If you expect auctions to be one of your main outlets for getting rid of fry, find out how often your local club holds them; some have auctions at every meeting, while others hold them only once or twice a year. You don't want to have your rearing tanks bursting with fry and several new batches on the way, and the next auction six months away.

These juvenile *Corydoras adolfoi* would probably sell very quickly in a fish club's auction.

Selling Them Through Classifieds Ads

As noted in Chapter 1, you're unlikely to get rich selling fish, but some people do make enough to help subsidize their fish addiction. That's particularly true if you're breeding fish that aren't easy to obtain locally. However, be aware that there are many hassles and expenses associated with shipping live fish. In addition to purchasing shipping bags, insulated boxes, and oxygen cylinders to pump air into the bags before shipping, you'll need to arrange with a delivery service to pick them up, or drop them off yourself at the shipping center, since you can't let fish sit in bags for an extended period of time. And speaking of shipping, it's expensive; a fish that sells for $5 can cost four times that much to ship, a differential that buyers won't be willing to pay if they can easily get the same species elsewhere. The bottom line is that before you commit yourself to direct-marketing fish, you must be certain you're willing to deal with the hassles involved, including buyers who become irate when something goes wrong, as it almost certainly will at some point.

Use As Feeder Fish

Cruel as it sounds, it's probably the most natural alternative, since in the wild, large numbers of fry would be eaten by other fish. Many species of captive fish rely on a steady diet of other fish, and their owners often prefer to obtain these feeder fish from hobbyists whose fishkeeping methods they trust, as opposed to pet shops where they may be exposed to overcrowded or disease-laden tanks.

Pros and Cons of Different Breeding Setups

Now that you've thought through some of the preliminary issues involved in a successful breeding operation, it's time to talk about the physical setup. There are three basic scenarios: You can breed fish in your community tank, breed them as a group in a single-species tank, or provide your breeding pair with a tank all to

Part 1

themselves. Each comes with built-in advantages and disadvantages; which one you choose will depend mostly on the needs of the species of fish you're trying to breed, but should also take into account what you're trying to accomplish with your breeding program, and the time and energy you have to put into it.

Community Tanks

It's not always necessary to create a special environment to get your fish to reproduce. Some, such as guppies, platys, and swordtails, will breed in almost any setup, including community tanks. As long as the fish you're trying to breed don't require specialized spawning conditions (such as a higher- or lower-than-normal temperature) that would clash with the needs of their tankmates, you can simply leave them in your community tank and let them do what comes naturally.

You may need to add specific items, however, such as a spawning grate (see the equipment section) or extra plants, to encourage the fish to breed or to prevent the fry from being cannibalized by tankmates or their own parents. Alternatively, if you're breeding livebearers and are present when the fry are born, you can catch and transfer them to a rearing tank.

Ruby Barbs will commonly spawn in community aquariums.

Pros: Your breeding pairs aren't stressed by being netted and transferred to another tank; in addition, you don't have to go to the time and expense of setting up and maintaining another tank. If you simply want the fun of breeding a few fish once in a while, this setup might be a good one for you. It works particularly well for livebearers and other easy-to-breed species such as Zebra Danios, as long as you have a way to protect the eggs and/or fry. In addition, mouthbrooders are sometimes bred in community settings, since they hold on to their fry until they're big enough to survive on their own.

Cons: You'll have far fewer surviving fry—in some cases, only a couple—since other fish in your tank will consider both eggs and fry to be tasty tidbits. (In fact, when a livebearing fish goes into labor, tankmates often cluster around her, waiting for fry to emerge so they can gobble them up.) You can save most of the babies by putting the female in a breeding trap (see equipment section) shortly before she delivers. Providing a thicket of real or silk plants or even floating plastic plants will also enable some of the fry to hide from their tankmates, but many of them may inevitably be eaten anyway, so you should check the tank daily for fry and remove them to a rearing tank for their own safety. In a community setting with several males and females of the same species, you'll have less control over which fish mate with one another, so if you're trying to selectively breed fish to emphasize certain traits, such as color or fin shape, then the community-tank approach isn't for you.

Breeding Tanks

The opposite of the community-tank approach, these are tanks designed to meet the spawning needs of particular fish. Fish are

Breeding tanks are usually best kept simple and functional.

sometimes conditioned for breeding in a community tank, and then transferred to the breeding tank for spawning.

Pros: Because you only have to worry about the needs of one pair (or in some cases, a small group) of fish, you can cater to their spawning preferences, thereby maximizing your chances of breeding them successfully.

Cons: There can be a fair amount of both time and expense involved in setting up and maintaining a breeding tank; you'll need not only the tank (or tanks) but a hood, stand, heater, and filter, plus whatever specific pieces of equipment are required by the species you're trying to breed. And did we mention that you'll also need space for all of the above? You'll also have to net your breeding pairs to transfer them to the new tank, something that can be stressful for both fish and keeper.

Species Tanks

A cross between a community and a breeding setup, a species tank was the most common way of breeding fish in the early days of the hobby. In this setup, a same-species group of fish is kept in a single tank, and several generations of their offspring grow up and breed together. Such setups work well for livebearers, as well as species such as danios that prefer to spawn in groups. Some breeders who use species tanks divide them into zones, planting one area densely as a sort of "maternity" and fry-raising area, while leaving plenty of open swimming area for the other fish.

A species tank will offer the best chances of breeding and raising fishes like these Black Arowanas.

Pros: Like breeding tanks, species tanks enable you to control the environment– water, temperature, etc.–to meet the needs of the species you're trying to breed without worrying about whether those needs clash with other fish in the tank. It usually involves less work than a breeding setup, since you can leave the fish in their environment instead of creating an entirely new one just to spawn them. You'll be able to observe the emergence of social hierarchies as well as the mate-selection process.

Cons: Some of the drawbacks of the community tank apply. If you want a high yield of fry, you may have to remove the eggs (or the fry, in the case of livebearers) to prevent them from being eaten. And since the fish will pick their own mates, you won't be able to selectively mate them to enhance particular characteristics in their fry. Species tanks are also inappropriate for some aggressive fish, such as Oscars or bettas, since they generally are don't tolerate same-sex members of their own species.

Planning The Physical Setup

The main purpose of a display tank is to show off your fish and the various elements that go into it–substrate, plants, and decorations– are chosen with that in mind. The purpose of a spawning or rearing tank, on the other hand, is utilitarian, and the décor is meaningful only to the extent that it meets the needs of the fish you're trying to breed or raise in the tank. In other words, breeding and rearing tanks don't have to look nice; they just have to get the job done. The following are some of things you will have to take into consideration.

Aquariums

If you decide not to breed your fish in a community or species setup, you will need at least one extra tank and probably two or more (sometimes many more!) in order to spawn the adults and raise the fry.

A lot of planning and cost will be needed to produce a breeding setup like this one.

Spawning Tanks

The size of the spawning (or breeding) tank you choose should depend on the species you're trying to breed, taking into account not just the size of the fish but its breeding habits and the swimming room it requires. (Fast-moving species generally need larger tanks than equivalently-sized slow swimmers, for instance.) Regardless of size, tanks that are low and wide (such as a 20- or 30-gallon long) make better breeding tanks than tall, narrow show

Part 1

tanks, because they permit more gas exchange at the water's surface. Breeding tanks should also have covers, since fish often chase one another vigorously while courting, and have been known to jump out of uncovered tanks.

Rearing Tanks

Sometimes also referred to as grow-out tanks, these are essentially nurseries for fry. Like human infants, baby fish are far more sensitive to environmental conditions than their adult counterparts, and keeping them in a separate tank allows you to more precisely control the quality of their water. (It also protects them from adult fish that might eat them.) In rearing tanks, bigger is not always better, at least in the first week or two after fry become free swimming, since in very large tanks it is sometimes difficult for them to track down food. Many breeders start fry out in a small tank—or even mason jars, for the tiniest fry—and move them to larger quarters as they grow. If you are raising more than a handful of fry, you are likely to need multiple rearing tanks, since a 10-gallon aquarium that can handle 100 two-day-old fry will be able to fit only a fraction of that number by the time those same fry are two months old. (If you live in a small apartment with little free space for tanks, you might want to consider breeding some of the less-prolific fish!) Rearing tanks usually have bare bottoms to make it easier to siphon out fish waste and leftover food, and rarely have plants or décor, but they should have covers, especially if you're raising anabantoids; if the air at the surface of the water isn't warm and moist, the labyrinth organs of the fry may be damaged.

Even temporary power filters can suck up large numbers of fry.

Filtration

Filtration is at least as important–if not more so–in breeding and rearing tanks than it is in other types of setups; it's just a little trickier to deal with. On the one hand, a filter is important for maintaining water quality. On the other, it can interfere with fertilization by drawing in eggs and/or milt. In addition, power filters can agitate the surface of the water, disrupting the spawning process in fishes such as bettas and gouramis since they build bubble nests. The easiest solution is to use a sponge filter in your breeding tanks, and/or shut the filter off during the actual spawning.

In rearing tanks, all but the gentlest of filters can suck in fry. For that reason, some breeders skip them altogether, relying on water changes to maintain water quality until the fry are strong enough swimmers to avoid the currents created by filters. Alternatively, they use sponge filters set on a very slow bubble.

Some breeders paint the outside of the bottom of their breeding tanks a dark color because it seems to make skittish fish feel more secure.

Substrate

Like just about every other component of

a breeding setup, the substrate you choose–if any–depends on the species of fish you're trying to spawn. Pit nesters, for instance, need sand or fine gravel in which to dig their nests, but many other species require no substrate at all.

Substrate can also serve a protective function. Many breeders place a double layer of glass marbles or coarse gravel on the bottom of tanks in which they plan to breed egg scatterers; the eggs drift down into it, out of the reach of the adult fish that might otherwise eat them. They can then hatch in safety. As mentioned, fry tanks typically do not have substrate.

Location

Where you place your tank can sometimes affect your fish's willingness to spawn in it. For instance, skittish fish may be too nervous to breed if their tank is located in a high-traffic area, and fish that are triggered to spawn by morning sun will breed more readily if you position the tank where it will get some natural light. Still others, such as tetras, prefer darker locations, and will be less likely to breed in a tank that gets direct sun.

Lighting

In display tanks, lighting makes it easier to view the fish. In breeding tanks, it serves a more utilitarian purpose, by mimicking the day-night cycles that serve as breeding triggers for some species. Certain African cichlids, for instance, can sometimes be coaxed to breed by adjusting the tank lighting to reflect the longer hours of daylight that occur in the summer. Putting the lights on a timer makes this simple.

This spawning mop has served its purpose well. Look closely and you will see the tiny eggs of a rainbowfish!

Plants and Plant Substitutes

Plants can serve a number of purposes in a breeding tank. They help to maintain water quality by taking in carbon dioxide and giving off oxygen. They can provide spawning sites for plant-choosing egg depositors such as rainbowfish, are incorporated into nests by fish such as dwarf gouramis, and provide hiding places for females that are at risk of being injured by the aggressive behavior of courting males. In addition, thick foliage can provide hiding places for fry in community and species tanks. If the tank will not have substrate in which to root plants, they can be placed in the tank in pots.

It is a good idea to disinfect the plants carefully before placing them into the breeding tank, since they can introduce bacteria and organisms that can harm the eggs. Alternatively, yarn tassels known as spawning mops can be placed in the tank as a substitute for plants. They are easy to make, and can be sterilized by boiling--an advantage over real plants!

Aeration

In display tanks, power filters often provide an aerating function, stirring up the surface of the water and facilitating gas exchange—the process by which atmospheric oxygen enters the water and gases such as carbon dioxide are released. In breeding and rearing tanks, however, the extremely gentle filtration makes the process less efficient, so many breeders compensate by using air pumps and airstones. This is particularly important in tanks where eggs are being incubated, since insufficient oxygen in the water can allow fungus to grow on the eggs.

Spawning Sites

Some fish are downright finicky about where they lay their eggs. Angelfish, for instance, like flat, almost vertical surfaces, while many rainbowfish require thickets of vegetation. The specifics for individual species are discussed in Part 2 of this book, but some typical spawning sites include plants (real or artificial), rocks, pieces of slate, commercially available spawning cones (conical terracotta structures with a trough at the bottom to catch the eggs), caves, shells (if you're breeding shell-dwelling cichlids), and the substrate itself.

Oscar pairs usually aren't picky about where they spawn as long as they can't see other fish.

Temperature Control

A reliable heater with a built-in thermostat is essential for breeding tropical fish, since water temperature plays such an important role in both spawning and rearing of the fry. Many professional breeders heat their tank room instead of the water, but this is less practical for small-scale home breeders because of the costs involved. A submersible heater with an easy-to-adjust thermostat is a bonus, since you may have to change the water temperature to trigger spawning in some species.

Part 1

Neothauma shells are commonly used as a spawning site for most shell-dwelling cichlids.

A male Neolamprologus ocellatus defending a shell containing his mate and their spawn.

Hiding Places

There are two reasons to provide hiding places in a breeding tank: First, males of many species of fish become quite aggressive toward females during or immediately after spawning, so it's important to provide females with places to escape if things are getting too rough. In addition, some species of fish, such the shell-dwelling cichlids of Lake Tanganyika, will only spawn in enclosed places. Hiding places don't have to be fancy; they can consist of strategically placed plants or rocks, pieces of PVC pipe set on the bottom or suspended horizontally from the side of the tank with string or wire, terracotta flowerpots placed on their sides or upside down with a hole knocked into the side, hollowed-out coconut halves with "doors" cut into them, and caves made from rock or resin.

Other Equipment

There is a wide assortment of other equipment that will often make your experiences with spawning and raising fishes more enjoyable. Be creative and don't be afraid to try new things. You never know, sometimes the smallest adjustment can reap large rewards.

Breeding Traps

These are nets or plastic cages that are used to separate breeding pairs, pregnant females, and sometimes eggs or fry from the rest of the population in a tank. There are many designs, the earliest of which was a funnel in a jar; the fry could swim through the small hole and escape the mother, who was too large to follow. More modern breeding traps often have perforated grates in the bottom, enabling fertilized eggs to fall through them to safety. Despite the name, the least-practical use of a breeding trap is for spawning, since many fish feel too cramped to breed in its confined quarters. More often, a pregnant livebearer is placed in a breeding trap shortly before delivery, to protect her fry from becoming snacks for other fish in the tank. The drawback is that being in the trap is stressful for the mother-to-

Breeding traps are an essential and fun piece of equipment for raising livebearers.

Plastic grating is usually available from hardware stores.

be, and can sometimes cause her to lose her fry, especially when she's transferred too early.

Spawning Grates

These are similar to the grates in some breeding traps, except that they are placed in the bottom of the tank itself. The fertilized eggs drift through the holes in the grate, hatching beneath it in safety, out of reach of adult fish that might eat them. Although they are sometimes available commercially, many breeders make their own from "egg crating" (plastic grids used to protect fluorescent ceiling lights, available in home-supply stores) or the perforated plastic mesh used for needlework.

Tank Dividers

These are glass, mesh, or acrylic screens that can be placed in a tank to divide it vertically. They can be used to keep males and females separate during conditioning; they can also provide a refuge for females if you cut a hole in one big enough for her to pass through, but too small for the male to follow. And a mesh divider placed across a darkened portion of the tank can serve as a vertical spawning grate; the adults spawn in the dark side, and their fry, drawn to the light, swim through the grate to safety. Tank dividers can be purchased, but also can be made from pieces of acrylic or egg crating cut to size and glued into place using aquarium-safe silicone. Alternatively, you can use the perforated plastic sheets made for needlepoint; slide the sides into plastic report binders and then wedge or glue them into your tank with silicone.

How to Make a Spawning Mop

Materials:

- A small ball of dark-colored acrylic or nylon yarn. (Don't use wool or cotton, which can rot and/or bleed.)
- An empty 35mm film canister.
- Aquarium gravel (if you want the mop to sink).
- Scissors.
- A hardcover book or piece of cardboard 8 to 10 inches long.

Methods:

1. Wrap yarn vertically around the book 20 to 30 times.
2. Cut another piece of yarn about a foot in length, and slide it between the cover of the book and the wrapped yarn. Tie it in an overhand knot, leaving the ends free.
3. Using the scissors, cut through the yarn directly opposite the knot, so both sides of the resulting tassel are equal.
4. If you want the mop to sink, pack gravel into the film canister; if you want it to float, leave it empty.
5. Put the ends of the yarn tie into the canister and pop the lid on to complete the mop.

Courtesy of Joe Graffagnino, Brooklyn Aquarium Society.

Plants help to oxygenate the water and take up excess carbon dioxide. They also provide spawning sites for fish. Here are some good plants for breeding tanks.

Broad-leafed plants (for species that like to lay their eggs on flat surfaces):
Echinodorus bleheri
Cryptocoryne spp.
Anubias barteri

Fine-leafed plants (for fish that spawn in plants, as well as bubble nesters; can also provide hiding places for fry):
Ceratophyllum demersum
Ceratopteris thalictroides
Hygrophila difformis
Cabomba caroliniana

Floating plants (for bubble nesters and to provide shy fish with a sense of security):
Salvinia spp.
Pistia stratiotes
Lemna minor

Plants that provide fry protection:
Bolbitis heudelotii
Vesicularia dubyana

Diet and Nutrition for Adult Fish

Healthy fry start with healthy brood stock–and you won't have healthy broodstock unless you feed them a good diet. Adult fish that are nutritionally deficient will be less likely to spawn, and those that do may have fewer offspring or produce eggs that don't hatch.

However, figuring out what constitutes a good diet isn't

Healthy broodstock is the result of good water conditions, good genetics, and a good diet.

always simple, because different species of fish have different dietary needs. Many plecos, for instance, are herbivores, and have extra-long digestive tracts that enable them to break down the fiber in their plant-based diet. They're not built to handle huge amounts of protein, and their health would suffer if that were all you fed them. The same thing would be true if you fed only plant-based food to infamous carnivores, like piranhas.

Manufacturers of prepared fish foods address this by creating specialized formulas and by including a balance of ingredients in the wafers, pellets, and flakes that make up the bulk of most aquarium fishes' diet. From an aquarist's point of view, such products come with many built-in advantages: They're widely available, relatively inexpensive, and for the time-pressed or squeamish, they're a lot easier and less messy than feeding, say, chopped earthworms.

The problem is that prepared foods contain more than just the vitamins, carbohydrates, fiber, and other substances fish need to stay healthy. Like processed foods consumed by humans, processed foods for fish also contain things like fillers, binders, and dyes, and flavors that aren't found in a fish's natural diet but are either necessary to the manufacturing process or designed to make the product more appealing to fish.

Although manufacturers insist their products contain all the nutrients fish need for optimal health, many experienced fishkeepers say that if commercial foods are all you feed your fish, they probably won't thrive. Instead, feed them a varied diet consisting of both a good-quality commercial food and live foods such as brine shrimp and mosquito larvae. By feeding a combination of things, you'll ensure that what your fish don't get from one food, they'll get from another.

Conditioning: Getting Your Fish in the Mood

Now that you know something about everyday fish nutrition, let's talk about the specialized role that food plays in the breeding process. While some species of aquarium fish—guppies and zebra danios, for instance—will reproduce in almost any situation, you will need to give many other species a little extra nudge by doing what is known as *conditioning* them—that is, preparing them for spawning by getting them into top physical shape. And diet plays an enormous role in that.

In the wild, such conditioning occurs naturally, often on a predictable schedule linked to annual climactic shifts. Warm weather, for instance, typically brings a boom in the worms, insects, crustaceans, protozoa, and algae that are present in water, providing a veritable smorgasbord for fish.

Since there is no rainy season to bring about such a change in the food supply in a home aquarium, you will have to take over nature's

These young Chocolate Cichlids are beginning to spar.

role by supplementing your fishes' diet with small but frequent meals of a wide variety of live foods. Eating these highly nutritious foods not only gives fish increased energy but stimulates production of healthy eggs and sperm. The sudden infusion of food may also signal to them that it is a good time to breed, because there will be plenty for their fry to eat. And some scientists theorize that the excitement of hunting down food as they would in the wild provides fish with the extra stimulation they need to spawn in captivity.

A pair of Curviceps guarding their clutch is always a welcome sight to see.

There are a couple of drawbacks to live food, however. First, getting hold of it is usually not nearly as convenient as running to the local pet shop and buying a can of flakes. Some pet shops carry live fish foods, and if you live near a bait shop, you may be able to buy some types there as well. But it's more likely that you'll have to catch, dig up, or culture live foods yourself–something that doesn't always go over well with other members of the family when they fling open the refrigerator door to discover a batch of squirming tubifex worms next to the lamb chops.

In addition, live foods can, in some instances, introduce parasites or other harmful organisms into your tank, particularly when collected in the wild. The alternative is to use a frozen or freeze-dried version of the live food; while the nutrient content may be slightly diminished by the processing, some breeders feel it's worth it because it's safer. If you do use live food, be sure the source from which you gather it (or buy it) is trustworthy.

Together or Separate?

Males and females can be conditioned together or separately, either by placing a divider in their tank or by moving them into separate quarters. The approach should depend on both the species you're trying to breed and your goals as a breeder. It is often better to separately condition males of aggressive species to prevent them from harassing the females during the pre-spawning period. In addition, separate conditioning allows you to eliminate unwanted reproduction by controlling the encounter between male and female. There's also an element of absence making the heart grow fonder: Males who are conditioned by themselves often go into spawning mode immediately when a female appears. Barbs and goldfish are examples of fish that are often conditioned separately.

On the other hand, fish–such as angelfish and discus–that form strong pair bonds should be conditioned together to keep that bond strong. When ready, they'll often spawn sponta-neously, without extra inter-vention on the part of the breeder.

Bonding is instilled in young Discus at a very early stage.

As an added note, there is some debate as to exactly what constitutes "conditioning separately." Some breeders simply place a partition in their tank; they believe that because fish are highly responsive to visual clues, being able to see one another helps to stimulate them. (So much so, apparently, that there are reports of mouthbrooding cichlids managing to breed even though they were on opposite sides of a perforated partition.) Other breeders, however, prefer the "out of sight, out of mind" approach, because they believe that being able to see one another may over stimulate the breeding pair, with the male frantically trying to get to the female, and the female becoming so eager to breed that she drops her eggs. If this does happen, continue conditioning, and she is likely to develop more eggs.

Perhaps the best advice is to try both approaches and see which one works best for you.

How Long to Condition

Once again, it depends on the species, and sometimes on the individual fish. Begin conditioning easy-to-breed fish at least a week before you hope to spawn them. Harder-to-breed fish may require several weeks to a month of live food in order to bring them into condition for spawning.

At first, it may be difficult to determine when your fish are in peak breeding condition, but with practice, you will become more skilled. Observe them closely during the conditioning period; brighter colors in the males and plumpness in the females (caused by a belly full of eggs) are signs that your fish are ready to spawn.

If you are conditioning them within view of one another, they may display some courtship behaviors as well.

Live Foods and How to Culture Them

Culturing live foods is a little like cooking: Just as there are many ways to make any given dish, there are many ways to culture live foods for your fish. So while the directions given here have worked for many aquarists, if they don't seem to produce a sufficient yield of live food for you, you may need to tinker with them a bit – storing your grindal worms at a slightly warmer temperature, for instance, or feeding your white worms potato chunks instead of baby cereal.

Brine Shrimp (Artemia)

Live brine shrimp are highly nutritious and universal favorite of hobbyists to feed their aquarium fish. They are available at many aquarium stores, or can be easily hatched at home using purchased brine-shrimp eggs (see box). There are also frozen and freeze-dried forms available.

The vibrant colors of these brine shrimp indicate that they're very healthy.

Bloodworms

The larvae of midge flies, these worms take their name from their deep red color. Fish love them, and in the wild, bloodworms are a staple in the diet of many species. They're also highly nutritious, and

How to Hatch Brine Shrimp

Materials:

- A clear 2-liter plastic bottle, such as a soda bottle, thoroughly rinsed
- Airline tubing, 3/16 in diameter and at least 2 feet long
- An air pump
- A lamp
- An extra piece of tubing to use as a siphon
- A brine shrimp net
- 1 tsp. brine shrimp eggs (available at your local aquarium shop)
- 2 tbsp. synthetic sea salt

Methods:

1. Fill the bottle with tap water to about an inch below the top. Add the sea salt and allow it to dissolve, then add the eggs.

2. Thread the tubing into the bottle until it is nearly touching the bottom. Turn on the pump to circulate the water, making sure the eggs are tumbling gently and continuously.

3. Place the bottle near the light to keep the water warm. The eggs will hatch in 24 to 36 hours, depending on water temperature. Plan to use them within a day, or they will consume their yolk sacs and their nutritional value will decline.

To use:

Remove the airline tubing and place the bottle near an incandescent light. Wait about 20 minutes for unhatched eggs and shells to settle out. The live shrimp will gravitate toward the light, making it easy to siphon them into a brine-shrimp net. Rinse and feed.

some studies suggest that fish whose diets are supplemented with blood worms grow better and have higher spawning rates. Efforts to culture bloodworms have been largely unsuccessful, so if you want to feed them to your fish, you'll have to either collect them in the wild by sieving the mud at the bottom of ponds, or buy frozen or freeze-dried varieties. Bloodworms are very rich, and some aquarists believe they should be used only as an occasional treat, because the overfeeding them has been linked to constipation.

Daphnia

Also known as water fleas, *Daphnia* are actually tiny crustaceans that contain large amounts of vitamins A and D as well as constipation-preventing roughage. (For this reason, many hobbyists offer them to their fishes even when they are not trying to condition their fish for breeding.) They are rarely available commercially, but can be collected in the wild by sieving the surface of ponds with a fine-mesh net or a turkey baster.

With difficulty, *Daphnia* can also be cultured at home. Start with a large, shallow container, such as a child's wading pool, filled to a depth of no more than a foot. Add a green-water culture that has been allowed to develop until it is emerald in color. Float a bag of *Daphnia* culture, available from a bio-supply company, in the wading pool for 15 minutes, just as you would to acclimatize fish. Then add the *Daphnia* to the pool very gradually. Some people also recommend adding a pump and airline to keep the water circulating.

Live *Daphnia* are an excellent conditioning food when available.

These small crustaceans feed readily on yeast and algae, among other things. The trickiest part is making sure they have enough to eat, but not so much that leftover food pollutes the water; they are very sensitive to water quality and will die off in massive numbers at the slightest hint of a problem. For this reason, many people keep several cultures going at a time. *Daphnia* can be harvested with a brine shrimp net or a piece of pantyhose and should be rinsed with dechlorinated water before feeding. An easier alternative to culturing: frozen or freeze-dried daphnia, which are widely available commercially.

Earthworms

Larger fish, such as goldfish, can be conditioned on chopped up earthworms. You can buy these from a bait shop or dig them up yourself, but if you choose the latter, make sure you take them from an area that you know to be pesticide-free.

Many larger fishes will appreciate occasional feedings of earthworms.

Grindal Worms

Smaller than but nutritionally similar to the white worms described later in this section, grindal worms can easily be cultured at home. Start with a small, waterproof container such as a plastic bait or shoe box, an ice cream container, or one of the Styrofoam boxes used to ship fish. Fill it two-thirds of the way with commercial potting soil (if you prefer to use dirt or compost from your yard, sterilize it in the microwave before using it) and mist it with water until it is damp but not drenched. Add a worm culture (available from a biological supply company or other hobbyists) and lightly sprinkle the soil with flaked baby cereal or cooked white rice. Cover the box loosely, since the worms need to breathe, and put it in a warm (68°-75°F), damp place, checking it daily. Re-mist the soil if it becomes too dry, and replace the baby cereal as it disappears, removing any that has become moldy. Within a week or two, you'll notice clumps of worms beginning to appear on the surface of the soil and on the sides of the container. Use tweezers to harvest them, or place a chunk of potato into the culture box; by the next day, it will be covered with worms, which can be harvested by dunking the chunk into a cup of water, then straining the water through a net. Rinse before feeding. Some aquarists add grindal worms directly to the tank; if it is aerated, they will circulate for a while in the water column. But others prefer to dispense them in a worm feeder, since grindal worms are capable of burrowing into the gravel substrate where fish can't get them. When they die, they pollute the water.

Mosquito Larvae

Humans hate mosquitoes, but fish love them–or at least their larvae. During the warm months, they can be found in almost any standing body of water, from puddles to birdbaths to ponds. To collect them, simply troll the area with a brine shrimp net or other piece of fine net. If you prefer to culture them yourself (and if the neighbors won't hate you), set a shallow container with a large surface area in a location that will receive some shade. Fill it with dechlorinated tap water and add a few chunks of fruits or vegetables, such as apples or lettuce. (You can bundle them in a piece of pantyhose to make them easier to remove later.) In about a week, the container should be filled with mosquito larvae, which resemble little threads hanging vertically just beneath the surface of

Part 1

the water. Strain the water through a coffee filter or another piece of pantyhose to collect the larvae. Just don't put so many in your tank that the fish can't eat them all, or what was supposed to be a meal for them may grow up and make a meal out of you!

Blackworms are often used as an alternate food in place of tubifex worms.

Tubifex Worms

These threadlike aquatic worms can grow to be an inch or more in length. Although fish love them, many breeders shunned them in the past because they grow in sludgy, polluted water, particularly near the outflow pipes of sewage treatment plants. As a result, they sometimes carried parasites and other pathogens that could be passed to humans as well as to fish. However, they are also highly nutritious; some studies indicate that fish conditioned on tubifex worms will have larger, healthier broods, and may even remain fertile longer. Because of concerns over pathogens, live tubifex can be difficult to obtain commercially; however, most pet shops carry freeze-dried and frozen versions that are guaranteed pathogen-free. You can also culture tubifex using shallow pans of water and worm culture available from biological supply companies; they can then be stored for several weeks in a pan of water in the refrigerator, as long as you change the water daily. Dispense them to your fish in a worm cone; if you simply dump them into the tank, they may flee to the bottom and tunnel under the gravel where fish can't reach them. Tubifex are an essential part of conditioning some aquarium fish, including discus.

Mbuna, like these Kenyi Cichlids, will appreciate regular offer-ings of veggie-based foods.

Vegetables

Fish that subsist largely on vegetable matter should be conditioned with it, too. Blanched lettuce, spinach, peas, and zucchini are good choices, as are cucumber slices (remove the seeds first to prevent them from floating around the tank). You can bind the vegetables to a rock using a rubber band, or use a plastic vegetable clip (available at an aquarium shop) to attach small pieces to the side of the tank.

White Worms

These segmented round worms are a good source of protein and fat and are often used to condition most fish. White worms live in damp soil and can often be found in large quantity in compost heaps or piles of wet and decaying leaves. They can also be cultured following the directions for grindal worms (above). However, store the culture box in a cooler place–white worms seem to reproduce best at a temperature of about 60°F. Use tweezers to harvest them, and rinse thoroughly before feeding them to fish. Because of their fat content, and the fact that fish love them so much that they tend to gorge on them, some breeders advise feeding them no more than twice a week; otherwise, fish could become obese.

The Role of Commercial Foods in Conditioning Fish

Prepared foods may have their limitations, but that doesn't mean you should stop offering them to your fishes completely, even during the conditioning process. Because they contain a wide array of nutrients, many aquarists feed prepared foods to their brood stock twice daily during conditioning, supplementing it with several smaller feedings of live foods throughout the day.

A Note on Overfeeding

Beginning breeders, knowing fish must be well fed to get them in breeding shape, will often dramatically increase the quantity of food they give at each meal. Unfortunately, quantity does not equal quality, and rather than getting their fish in shape for spawning, such a strategy often does the opposite. Overfeeding can result in sluggish, overweight fish and health problems such as fatty liver disease, one of the most common killers of fish in captivity. And overweight fish won't have the energy needed to produce healthy broods—if they even have the energy to spawn.

Instead, feed fish small amounts of flake food–no more than the fish can eat in two minutes—once or twice a day, supplemented by small quantities of live foods two or three times a day.

Troubleshooting

If you have tried unsuccessfully to spawn a compatible pair of fish that you know to be of reproductive age, the problem may be timing. While some fish (particularly livebearers), can be bred in captivity all year long, other species seem to reproduce more reliably at certain times of the year. The reproductive rate of many

African cichlids falls to almost nothing in the winter (although they can sometimes be coaxed by setting tank lights to mimic a summer light cycle). And other fish, such as Red-Tailed Black sharks, seem to have their own internal spawning clocks, going months at a time without breeding, no matter how much conditioning they undergo.

5

Fry Care

There are few things more discouraging to a breeder than finally getting a favorite pair of fish to spawn, only to have all the fry die days or weeks later. Unfortunately, it's not an uncommon scenario–but it is one that an aquarist can often avoid if he or she has a good understanding of the special needs that fry have and is conscientious about meeting them.

Experienced parents will often take very good care of their brood.

Water Quality

Fry are far more sensitive to water quality than most adult fish, and even small amounts of ammonia or nitrites, or excessive levels of nitrates, can kill them or stunt their growth. So it's extremely important to make sure that the water quality in a rearing tank is as close to perfect as you can get it.

That means making sure you don't overstock or overfeed, and doing regular water changes–in other words, all the same things you do to maintain adult fish. It's just that with fry, it's a little more important to get the balance right.

Superior water quality on a continuous basis will be needed to raise baby Discus to adulthood.

That's because fry need lots of food to fuel their development. And lots of food equals lots of fish poop and other decomposing organic material in the water, which, untended, equal ammonia, nitrites, and nitrates in quantity.

The best way to prevent this, of course, is to do small but regular water changes, making sure to siphon out all the detritus from the bottom of the tank in the process. (That is one of the reasons rearing tanks rarely have substrate.) In a fry tank, it's not uncommon to change 10 to 25 percent of the water every day or every couple of days–being careful, of course, to match the pH, hardness, and temperature of the new water to that of the old, since fry are highly sensitive to changes in their environment.

Be careful, too, not to vacuum up fry, which can easily get caught in the pull generated by even a very small gravel vacuum. To protect them, take the "bell" off the end of the vacuum and just use the tubing, or for very small fry, use airline tubing. You can create an additional safety net for the fry–both literally and figuratively– by fitting a clean piece of nylon stocking or gauze over the end of the hose and fastening it with a rubber band.

A Word On Stocking Density

Studies have shown that fry kept in overstocked tanks are at risk of stunted growth and may never reach a normal adult size. In worst-case scenarios, overstocking can lead to outbreaks of bacterial disease, and even deaths of some or all of the fry. The problem is that the definition of "overstocked" changes as the fry grow: A 10-gallon tank may easily support hundreds of fry in their earliest stage of development, when they look like nothing more than snippets of thread with eyes. But as they get bigger, they will put an increasingly heavy load on the filter, which will in turn affect water quality. So be

Angels are very prolific and if they are overcrowded, they will often become disfigured.

prepared to move some of them to other tanks before this happens, and maybe even to repeat the process a couple of times before they're grown.

Feeding Fry

Would you feed a hamburger to a week-old infant? Of course not! Not only would the baby be physically unequipped to chew and digest it, but it wouldn't contain the right balance of nutrients necessary for his or her stage of development.

Like newborn humans, newborn fish need special foods, and plenty of them. Unlike adult fish, which can typically go a week or two without food, fry can starve to death within a day if they don't have enough to eat. And even if they do survive, malnourished fry probably won't grow well, and may develop problems such as curvature of the spine.

While you'll need to feed livebearer fry shortly after they're born, do not feed the fry of egg-laying species until they are *free swimming*–that is, able to swim on their own–something that usually takes a few days to a week after they hatch. Until then, the fry will remain stationary, feeding off the remnants of their *yolk sac*– a membrane-enclosed cocktail of fats, proteins, and other substances, visible as a pouch extending from their belly. But once they use this up, you will need to feed them several times a day.

From the outset, some fry, including those of most livebearers, will be big enough to eat regular flake food crushed into a powder. But fry of many other species are so small that the only things that

Part 1

they're able to fit in their mouths are microscopic organisms known as infusoria.

What follows are some common first foods for fry. Many call for starter cultures, which you can obtain either from a biological supply company (check the Internet) or from other hobbyists.

Commercial Fry Food

It is available in both liquid and powdered forms, and in formulas for livebearers and egg-layers. Fry food isn't just a ground-up version of the flakes fed to adult fish; rather, it has a nutritional balance that takes into account the accelerated growth rates of fry. Probably the easiest way to feed your fry, but some breeders claim fry fed exclusively on prepared foods will not grow as rapidly or be as robust as those fed a varied diet that includes live foods.

Green Water

This is just water with unicellular algae in it, often used as a first food for fry, as well as to culture daphnia and some other live foods. To make, fill a jar with tank water and set in a sunny location until the water turns green. You can also add small, smooth rocks, which will grow a coat of algae that can be used to feed plecostomus fry and other bottom-feeding herbivores.

Very small fry will do best if offered green water and infusoria as first foods.

Infusoria

This is a catchall name for microscopic organisms such as protozoa and unicellular algae, which provide an excellent first food for tiny fry. Culturing your own is simple: Place vegetable matter, such as a couple of crumpled leaves of lettuce (make sure it's pesticide-free) or a small chunk of boiled potato, in a jar and pour tank water over it. Set in a warm, dark place but do not cover, since the spores from which infusoria grow are airborne. Within a day or two, you'll notice that the water becomes cloudy as the infusoria begin to grow. This water can be added to the rearing tank with an eyedropper. Some breeders simply drop crushed lettuce leaves into the rearing tank as soon as the fry hatch; by the time they're free swimming, infusoria will have developed. The downside to this is that the decomposing lettuce leaves can pollute the water, so if you use this method, you'll need to monitor water quality carefully.

Baby Brine Shrimp (Naupulii)

This is one of the most nutritious foods for fry, and can be fed to all but the smallest of them. Instructions for culturing brine shrimp can be found in Chapter 4. Make sure that you use them within 24 hours of hatching (and preferably less), since the naupulii will use up their yolk sacs after that and their nutritional value will decrease.

Microworms

Another highly nutritious fry food that is easy to produce. Start by cooking a small quantity of regular unsalted oatmeal. Spread in a small plastic container, such as a margarine tub, to a depth of about half an inch, and cool to room temperature. Add a spoonful of worm culture and sprinkle lightly with baker's yeast. Within a few days, the culture will start to look soupy, an indication the worms are multiplying. To harvest, warm the container slightly by placing it under a lamp or on top of the tank light; within 20 minutes or so, the worms will begin climbing the sides of the container and can be scraped off with a spoon or your finger. Rinse and feed to fry with an eyedropper. One disadvantage of microworms is that they sink to the bottom of the tank, and surface-feeding fry sometimes have a hard time finding them.

Vinegar Eels

Despite the name, these aren't actually eels–they're nematodes that grow no larger than one-sixteenth of an inch. Their tiny size makes them an excellent first food for fry, and unlike microworms, they swim throughout the water column, making it easy for fry to find them. They're also easy to grow: All you have to do is fill a gallon container–a plastic milk jug, well rinsed, is fine–about two-thirds of the way with equal parts dechlorinated water and apple cider vinegar. Add half an apple sliced to fit through the neck of the bottle (it's not necessary to peel or core) and a vinegar-eel culture. Cover the mouth of the jar with cloth to let air in and keep other insects out, then store at room temperature. In about a month, if you hold the container up to a bright light and look closely, you'll see the eels, which resemble barely-visible slivers of glass. To harvest, pour the medium through a coffee filter and rinse in lukewarm tap water, then swish it in the fry tank. One advantage to feeding vinegar eels is that they can live in the tank for several days; in a pinch, you can put some in the tank in the morning and simultaneously supply your fry with breakfast, lunch, and dinner without worrying about the effect of decomposing food on water quality.

Bumble Bee Gobies will usually breed deep within small caves or shells.

Hard-Boiled Egg Yolk

Many prepared fry foods contain egg yolk, but you don't have to buy commercial foods to give your fish the benefits of this excellent protein source. Instead, wrap the yolk of a hard-boiled egg tightly in a fine-mesh cloth, dunk it in the tank, and squeeze it gently under water. This forces tiny particles of the yolk through the cloth and into the tank, where the fry can get them.

Incubating Eggs

After spawning, adult fish often try to eat their eggs. For this reason, it is usually advisable to remove one or the other from the tank. If removing the eggs, you can either siphon them out with airline tubing, or if they have been laid on a rock or plant or in a spawning mop, move the entire thing to the new tank.

A word of caution, however. Eggs, like fry, are often very sensitive to environmental changes. Make sure the water parameters of the new tank exactly match those of the spawning tank. In addition, eggs that have been moved seem more likely to grow fungus than those that remain in the breeding tank. To discourage this, move the eggs in a small container of water so they won't be exposed to the air. And once they're in the new tank, make sure water circulates gently around them. (Adding an airstone will help to achieve this.) Some aquarists also add a small quantity of acriflavine or methylene blue as a disinfectant. Use tweezers or a siphon to promptly remove eggs that grow fungus, to prevent it from spreading.

Stripping Mouthbrooders

For a variety of reasons, breeders sometimes remove eggs or fry from mouthbrooders before the end of the normal incubation period, a process known as *stripping*. The eggs or fry are then raised in a separate tank. It is a somewhat controversial practice, since it can be stressful for the adult fish; some critics also believe fry learn brooding and guarding behaviors from their parents in a process called *imprinting,* and may not do as good a job of caring for their own future offspring if deprived of the opportunity to witness this. But other breeders argue there is no evidence of that, and say that in their experience, "stripped" fry do as good a job of parenting as any other mouthbrooder. They also point out that mouthbrooding is itself stressful for the parent because he or

Female mouthbrooders should be placed in a recovery tank after being stripped of their eggs.

she is unable to eat while holding eggs or fry—often for a month or more at a stretch. Either way, there are many good reasons to strip mouthbrooders. Consider stripping if the mouthbrooding parent:

- has a history of swallowing the eggs;
- has a history of spitting out eggs or fry prematurely;
- has a history of refusing to spit out fry, holding on to them so long

that they die;

• is ill;

• is weak and emaciated from being unable to eat.

Culling

One of the most disagreeable parts of breeding fish is culling–the selective destruction of unwanted fry because they are of inferior quality or because there are too many of them for the aquarist to

10 Easy Steps to Stripping Mouthbrooders

1. Start by preparing a tank for the fry, or an incubator for the eggs.

2. Place a very large net or a mesh breeding trap in the tank to catch the eggs or fry as the female spits them out.

3. Net the female.

4. With a wet hand (never dry), pick her up and hold her loosely but firmly just behind the gills.

5. Tilt her head down over the net or breeding trap, preferably with her head underwater.

6. *Gently* open her mouth by pressing a narrow blunt object such as a plastic coffee stirrer, the round end of a toothpick, or a miniature screwdriver against her lower lip. She should spit out her eggs or fry, which will tumble into the breeding trap.

   Important: Do not insert the stripping tool more than an eighth of an inch or so into her mouth or you could injure her and damage the eggs or fry.

7. Repeat several times, until you are certain there are no more eggs or fry in her mouth.

8. Put the female back into the main tank. If she has become emaciated from holding her fry, you may wish to instead place her in a separate tank and feed her high-quality foods for a week or so until she recovers.

9. Transfer the eggs or fry to the incubator or rearing tank.

10. Monitor the incubator or rearing tank closely watching for any signs of egg fungus or other types of disease.

How to Pack Fish for Transportation

Whether you will be auctioning your fry at an aquarium club meeting or shipping them to other hobbyists halfway across the country, it is important to pack them correctly.

Stop feeding the fish 24 hours prior to packing so they pass most of their feces. This will help to minimize fouling of water in the shipping bag.

Use appropriately-sized plastic bags at least 3 ml thick that are specifically meant to hold fish. These can be obtained from a fish-supplies distributor, and sometimes from your local aquarium store. Do not use bags meant for food, because fish can become trapped in their square corners.

Fill each bag about a quarter of the way with clean, aged water the same temperature as that in the tank. Some breeders also like to add a conditioner to repair any damage to the fish's slime coat that may occur during netting.

Add fish, and fill the rest of the bag with air by running an airline from an air pump into it. There should be three to four times as much air as water in the bag. Never fill the bag by blowing it up like a balloon; this adds carbon dioxide, not oxygen, and will stress your fish. *Important: If fish are to spend more than a few hours in the bag, use pure oxygen from a cylinder instead of atmospheric air from the air pump.*

Tightly close the bag with a rubber band. To safeguard against leaks, double-bag the fish by sliding the first bag upside down into another one of the same size and sealing that one with a rubber band as well. Use a waterproof marker to write the species name of the fish, gender (if known), and spawning date on the bag.

Place the fish in an insulated container.

If the fish is to be shipped, check with your carrier as to any particular packing requirements. Note: Do not ship fish when it is extremely hot or extremely cold, since even within an insulated container, the temperature may change enough to affect their health.

raise. While the idea of destroying a living creature, especially a fish, is distressing to many aquarists, it's often a necessary–even natural– part of a good breeding program. Remember that in the wild, fry with physical defects would find it difficult to escape predators or compete for food. This is nature's way of ensuring that only the fittest grow up to pass their genes on to a new generation. In the home aquarium, culling serves the same purpose, preventing the weaker members of a brood from spawning and perpetuating their problems. In addition, culling frees up tank space for the remaining fry, something that enables them to grow faster and remain healthier.

Although culling can be carried out at any time, most fishkeepers designate specific times for it during the fry-rearing process. They often conduct an initial cull when the fry are two or three weeks old, eliminating any with extreme physical deformities. They then follow this with a second and sometimes a third cull weeks or even months later as the fry grow and less-obvious defects begin to manifest themselves.

Part Two

"Congratulations. It's a bottomfeeder."

Introduction to Popular Species

This section is designed to give you detailed instructions for breeding and raising 37 of the most popular species of freshwater aquarium fishes. Many of these can be found at your local aquarium shop or easily found through local or national clubs and organizations.

White Clouds are very popular and often easy to spawn under the right conditions.

But first, a bit of a disclaimer: Breeding fish, like keeping them, is one part science and one part art. Readers who come to this section looking for a magic formula are likely to be disappointed, since there are many, many factors that affect the likelihood that a particular species will reproduce in a particular aquarium–among them minute variations in water chemistry, temperature, diet, and age of the fish, not to mention their individual personalities and histories. Even experienced aquarists are sometimes frustrated by their inability to induce a given species to breed, especially when they meet another hobbyist who lives two towns away and can't get the same species to stop breeding!

All of that is to say that the instructions that follow are based on what has worked for many aquarists over many years (and where there are conflicting reports, that's indicated, too). But you may still have to experiment a little bit to get your own fish to spawn, especially when it comes to some of the fussier species. Raise the water temperature a degree or two; drop the pH or the water depth; condition a little longer, or try a bigger tank. Draw on your knowledge of your fish, their habits in the wild, and the conditions in your tanks. After all, that's the challenge of breeding fish–and the fun!

6

Livebearers

Livebearers–at least the ones most commonly available in pet shops–are among the easiest fish for beginners to breed. In fact, many aquarists say the problem is not inducing their livebearers to spawn, but rather figuring out what to do with all the fry they produce.

Platys are one of the most popular groups of all the livebearers.

Most livebearers aren't fussy about the conditions under which they breed, sometimes even spawning in the often bare, brightly lit tanks of pet shops. Nor do they require special water parameters or environmental triggers. They can be bred in a community or species tank, although without a tank divider or thick foliage to protect them, the fry are often eaten.

Aquarists interested in developing new color morphs or fin shapes often work with livebearers because of their prolificacy and the hardiness of their fry. Selective mating to enhance specific characteristics is beyond the scope of this book, but is something you may wish to keep in mind for the future.

Guppies

Scientific Name: *Poecilia reticulata.*

Ease of Breeding: Easy.

Introduction: Imported to Europe around the turn of the last century, guppies soon earned the nickname "millions fishes," a reference to their prolific breeding habits. Although the wild form is somewhat drab, guppies have been selectively bred to create an astonishing array of colors and patterns.

Sex Differences: Male guppies are smaller and more colorful than females.

Water Conditions: Hardness and pH are not critical but extremes should be avoided. Temperature should be between 75° and 82°F.

Equipment: No special equipment required for breeding, but to raise the fry, you'll need a rearing tank, or at least thick foliage in the main tank to shelter them from hungry tank-mates.

Conditioning and Triggers: Condition together or separately with brine shrimp, white worms, and mosquito larvae plus flake food for a week or two prior to spawning. Spawn in groups of one male and two or three females per male.

Spawning: The male spreads his fins and swims around the female in an elaborate pattern, then repeatedly touches his gonopodium to her vent to transfer sperm. The female gives birth four to six weeks later, depending on water temperature. (The higher the temperature, the shorter the gestation.) As the pregnancy progresses, the female develops a gravid spot, and when delivery is imminent, she may get a squared-off look to her belly, dart around the tank, become quieter than usual, or hide. If you plan to transfer her to a breeder's trap to give birth, do it now; if you move her too early, she may become stressed and lose her fry.

Brood Size: There have been reports of a single female giving birth to 150 to 200 fry, but broods of 20 to 100 are more common.

Fry Care: Baby guppies are coiled inside a membrane at birth, but immediately break free and swim toward the nearest light source, making them easy to net for transfer to a grow-out tank. If they'll remain in the main tank, provide plenty of hiding places, such as floating plants, to protect them from other fish. Feed liquid or powdered fry food formulated for livebearers, baby brine shrimp, and/or flake food crushed into powder. Guppies are capable of reproducing when they're only two months old, so if you don't want more fry, separate the sexes.

Platys and Swordtails

Scientific Name(s): *Xiphophorus maculatus* (Platy); *Xiphophorus hellerii* (Swordtail).

Ease of Breeding: Easy.

Introduction: These hardy, colorful fish were among the first tropical fish kept in aquaria, and remain very popular. Platys were first bred in captivity in Italy in the 1860s.

Sex Differences: The anal fin of mature males has been modified into a tube-like structure called a gonopodium. Male swordtails also have long, pointed projections on their tails.

Water Conditions: Not critical.

Equipment: No special equipment required for breeding, but parents eat their young, so provide lots of hiding places, or separate them from their parents after birth.

Conditioning and Triggers: Platys and Swordtails seem to reproduce under almost any conditions. However, conditioning them separately with live food, such as white worms, mosquito larvae, and brine shrimp, for a week or two before spawning may produce a better yield of fry.

Spawning: A male courts a female by fanning his fins and posturing in front of her, then latches his gonopodium to her vent to transfer sperm. Gestation is about 28 days. Shortly before giving birth, she'll develop a gravid spot; she also may hide or become quieter than usual. At this point, move her to a breeding trap to protect the fry, or place her in a birthing tank; if you remove her shortly after she gives birth, you can raise the fry in the same tank.

Brood Size: Anywhere from a few to 100 or more depending on the condition and size of the female.

Fry Care: If rearing fry in the main tank, provide them with plenty of plants or even floating plastic "fry hideouts" (available at pet shops) so they can escape hungry tankmates. Better yet, transfer them to a bare-bottomed grow-out tank equipped with a sponge filter and a heater. Feed at least four times daily for best growth; fry are large enough to eat regular flake food crushed into a powder, but also appreciate fresh or frozen baby brine shrimp, microworms, and/or commercial fry food. Fry are sensitive to water-quality problems; for optimal health and growth, change 10 to 25 percent of the water daily.

Special Notes: These species readily crossbreed, so keep them in separate tanks to avoid hybridization.

Species with Similar Breeding Habits: Mosquitofish *(Gambusia affinis)*.

Mollies

Scientific Name: *Poecilia sphenops;* also *Poecilia latipinna* (Sailfin Molly) and *Poecilia velifera* (Green Sailfin Molly).

Ease of Breeding: Easy.

Introduction: Mollies have been bred in captivity since the late 1800s. They come in a wide variety of colors and body shapes: black, orange, salt-and-pepper, balloon-bodied, lyre-tailed, and sailfinned—to name just a few. They tend to be a bit fussier about the conditions they're kept in, however, preferring brackish water to fresh, and a higher temperature than most community fish.

Sex Differences: Males have a gonopodium, although it may not develop until the fish is nearly a year old. Females tend to be plumper than the males.

Water Conditions: Mollies like water that is on the hard side, so add two tablespoons per gallon of marine salt mix to their tank water. The pH should be neutral to somewhat alkaline, with 8.0 being the upper end of the range. Temperature should be 78° to 82°F, with the higher temperature being preferable.

Equipment: Mollies will readily spawn in community aquaria. Keep them in as large a tank as possible, with 29 gallons being the minimum size; use good filtration and add plenty of plants to make the fish feel secure.

Conditioning and Triggers: Supplement feedings of flake food with blood worms, brine shrimp, and black worms as well as some vegetable matter. Change about 20 percent of the water daily.

Spawning: A male Molly courts aggressively, flirting and fanning his fins. It is unclear as to whether he fertilizes the female's eggs by latching onto her with his gonopodium or simply expelling sperm near her vent. Gestation is usually 40 to 80 days depending on species—shorter for short-finned molly varieties and longest for sailfins. As the pregnancy progresses, you may be able to see a gravid spot on the female if she is of a light color. As delivery draws near, the female may also begin hiding or hanging out by herself in plants in the tank. Fry are typically born early in the morning. Females tend to be stressed when confined in a breeding tank, so move her to a tank of her own shortly before birth, or permit her to deliver in the main tank; the fry can then be netted and transferred to a rearing tank.

Brood Size: Can be as many as 100, but a brood of 30 to 50 is more typical.

Fry Care: Feed a good-quality fry food, newly hatched brine shrimp, microworms, and other live foods, and if possible, some vegetable matter. Do not crowd fry into a too-small tank—a gallon of water per fry is about right. Water quality is very important; start with a sponge filter, but switch to a power filter when fry are a few weeks old. This will give them current to swim against, as well as helping to maintain water quality.

Part 2

7

Anabantoids

Anabantoids have long fascinated aquarists because of their ability to breathe atmospheric oxygen through an unusual maze-like structure known as a labyrinth organ, which acts like a primitive lung. The family of labyrinth fish includes some of the most popular species in the hobby, including Siamese fighting fish, dwarf gouramis, and

The Siamese Fighting Fish is easily the most recognized type of Anabantoid.

kissing gouramis—so named because members of the species often lock lips with one another. (Although ironically, scientists believe this to be a sign of aggression, not affection!)

When it comes to spawning, anabantoids employ one of two strategies. Nearly all of those readily available to hobbyists are bubble-nest builders, but a few, including a couple of species of bettas, are mouthbrooders. In either case, one of the parents – often the male–guards the eggs and young until they are free swimming.

Pearl Gourami

Scientific Name: *Trichogaster leeri*

Breeding Strategy: Bubble nester.

Ease of Breeding: Easy.

Introduction: These fish are considered by many aquarists to be among the most beautiful of the freshwater species. They can grow to 5 or more inches, and are generally peaceful—at least for gouramis!

Sex Differences: Males have red-orange breasts that get even more vivid when they are in breeding dress. In addition, their dorsal fins are long and pointed, while those of females are short and rounded.

Water Conditions: Hardness and pH not critical as long as they are not extreme. Temperature should be around 80°F. Some breeders recommend a water depth of about 8 inches.

Equipment: Some breeders spawn these fish in a 10-gallon tank, but a 20-gallon long would be better. Add a cover, heater, filter, and plenty of fine-leaved plants. Some breeders add the lid to a margarine container or a piece of Styrofoam sliced from the bottom of a cup as an anchor for the bubble nest. This anchor can be fastened to the side of the tank by a length of string or allowed to float free. Males can be aggressive during spawning, so make sure the tank has plenty of hiding places for the female.

Conditioning and Triggers: Condition separately with live foods such as brine shrimp for about two weeks. Some breeders say that gradually raising the temperature to as high as 87°F may trigger spawning.

Spawning: Put the female into the tank a few hours before the male, so he thinks he's in her territory and not the other way around. The male will build his bubble nest, which may be several inches in diameter. When it is done, the male will attempt to lure or prod the female under it. Sometimes she nibbles at him to indicate her willingness to spawn. When she is in position under the nest, he curls himself around her and flips her upside down as she releases eggs. Remove the female but leave the male to guard the nest.

Brood Size: About 300.

Fry Care: Fry hatch in about a day and become free swimming about four days after that. Remove the male at this time, and feed the fry infusoria or liquid fry food. When they are about two weeks old, add baby brine shrimp. Keep the tank covered so that the air above the surface of the water remains warm and humid, and do a partial water change every two to three days. About three weeks after hatching, add a sponge filter. As the fry grow, be prepared to move them to other tanks to avoid too high a stocking density in the rearing tank.

Species with Similar Breeding Habits: Blue Gourami, Gold Gourami, Opaline Gourami *(Trichogaster trichopterus);* Moonlight Gourami *(Trichogaster microlepis);* Snakeskin Gourami *(Trichogaster pectoralis).*

Paradise Fish

Scientific Name: *Macropodus opercularis*

Breeding Strategy: Bubble nester.

Ease of Breeding: Easy.

Introduction: Paradise Fish were among the first tropical fish to be kept— and bred—in captivity, making their appearance in home aquariums in Europe as early as the second half of the 19th century. Colorful, curious, and hardy, they remain favorites today.

Sex Differences: Males have longer fins and are more brightly colored than females.

Water Conditions: Not critical.

Equipment: Tank should be at least 10

gallons, with 20 being even better. These fish like to jump, so make sure the tank has a secure cover. If filtration is used, it should be minimal—a sponge filter set on a slow bubble—to avoid agitating the surface and disturbing the bubble nest. Add floating and/or fine-leaved plants, which the male will use to help anchor the nest. The plastic lid to a margarine tub or other such container can be floated in the tank to serve the same purpose. Tank should be covered to keep the air above it warm and humid.

Conditioning and Triggers: Condition with good-quality flake food supplemented with live and frozen foods such as brine shrimp. Some breeders report that raising the temperature in the tank by a couple of degrees and reducing the water level has triggered these fish to spawn.

Spawning: The male builds the bubble nest, then begins to display to the female, trying to lure her back to it. The female indicates her receptiveness by wriggling at him. The two then swim back to the nest and the female turns upside down under it as the male wraps his body around hers. They simultaneously release eggs and sperm; the fertilized eggs float up to the nest. Remove the female immediately after spawning so the male does not attack her in his efforts to protect the eggs.

Brood Size: Up to 500.

Fry Care: The male will aggressively guard the eggs until they hatch; at this point, he should be removed, because the fry are immediately free swimming, and he may try to eat them. Feed the fry infusoria and liquid fry food; after a week or two, add newly hatched brine shrimp. As they grow, you can add finely crushed flake food, microworms, and *Daphnia*.

Dwarf Gourami

Scientific Name: *Colisa lalia*

Breeding Strategy: Bubble nester.

Ease of Breeding: Easy.

Introduction: Native to India, Dwarf Gouramis are popular community-tank inhabitants because of their beautiful colors and generally peaceful nature. The biggest challenge in breeding them may be obtaining a female; the males are so much more colorful that many pet shops don't bother to stock the drabber females; you may have to special-order them.

Sex Differences: Male Dwarf Gouramis can be blue with red stripes or mostly red. Females are a silvery gray.

Water Conditions: Hardness and pH not critical. Temperature should be 75° to 81°F.

Equipment: A 10-gallon tank with hood, filled with 4 to 6 inches of water and a heater set to about 80°F. Thick vegetation will give the female a place to hide if the male becomes too aggressive; fine-leaved or floating plants such as *Riccia* make the breeding pair feel more secure, and males also incorporate pieces into their bubble nests. Some breeders report that male Dwarf Gouramis are willing to use a chunk of Styrofoam cut from a cup to anchor for their bubble nest.

Conditioning and Triggers: Separately condition the male and female with live and flake foods for about a week. Transfer the male to the breeding tank in the evening. Add the female the following morning.

Spawning: The male should soon begin building a bubble nest, if he has not already done so. It will be several inches across. The female watches, and when she is ready to spawn, she nudges the male and he wraps himself around her, turning her upside down as she releases eggs and he releases milt. The fertilized eggs drift downward, and the male retrieves them and spits them into the nest. Spawning often lasts between two to four hours. When complete, remove the female, but leave the male to guard the nest.

Brood Size: Between 300 and 800.

Fry Care: Fry will hatch within 12 to 24 hours, and become free swimming three days later. At this point, remove the male, or he may try to eat the fry. Feed the fry infusoria and/or commercial fry food for the first week; you can add newly hatched brine shrimp and pulverized flake food the week after that. Be sure to keep the rearing tank covered to keep the air above the water's surface warm and humid; otherwise, when the fry swim to the surface to breathe, their labyrinth organ may be damaged.

Species with Similar Breeding Habits: Honey gourami (*Colisa chuna).*

Betta

Scientific Name: *Betta splendens*

Breeding Strategy: Bubble nester.

Ease of Breeding: Easy, but raising fry can be challenging.

Water Conditions: Hardness and pH not critical. Temperature should be about 80°F.

Sex Differences: Most captive-bred males have long, flowing fins, while females have short fins and a pimple-like white bump below their vents.

Equipment: A 5- or 10-gallon tank with a cover, filled with 4 to 6 inches of water.

Add floating plants or a piece of a Styrofoam cup as an anchor for the bubble nest, and plants or rocks as hiding places for the female if the male becomes too aggressive.

Conditioning and Triggers: Condition males and females in separate bowls, feeding grindal and white worms and good-quality commercial food for about a week. When the female is plump with eggs, place the male in the breeding tank and the female in a floating container in the same tank. The male should begin building a bubble nest and flaring. When the female's breeding stripes become evident and she indicates interest by flaring back or pointing head down in the container, release her.

Spawning: The male lures the female to the nest and folds himself around her. As she releases eggs, which resemble grains of salt, he gathers them in his mouth and spits them into the nest. When spawning is complete, remove the female, but leave the male to guard the eggs.

Brood Size: About 100.

Fry Care: The fry hatch in one to three days, and become free swimming about three days after that. Remove the male at this point, and feed the fry infusoria or specialty fry food, vinegar eels, or microworms. Add baby brine shrimp after a week. When fry are two weeks old, increase the water level an inch at a time. Some breeders suggest separating males as soon as they can be sexed, while others say males raised together will not fight.

Special Notes: Many Bettas stop spawning by the time they're 14 months old—important to know, since most are a year old by the time they reach pet shops. Better option: Buy a pair of juveniles directly from another breeder. Some suggest the female be the same size or smaller than the male; if she's bigger, she may bully him.

Chocolate Gourami

Scientific Name: *Sphaerichthys osphromenoides*

Breeding Strategy: Mouthbrooder.

Ease of Breeding: Extremely difficult to breed, as well as to raise the fry.

Introduction: These beautiful brown-and-cream striped gouramis, native to Malaysia and Sumatra, are very difficult to keep, not to mention breed. It is a species to aspire to once you've mastered breeding most other types of fish.

Sex Differences: Females are larger and thicker than males, which are more brightly colored.

Water Conditions: Start with a pH of between 5 and 6.5 and a dH of 0 to 5; temperature should be between 75° and 82°F, with the upper end of that range being preferable. Water quality is critical; do 15 percent changes every week.

Equipment: This species can be spawned in a species tank of at least 50 gallons or as a breeding group of one male and three or four females in a tank of at least 25 gallons.

In either case, place it in a quiet location with dim lighting. Add a heater and a cover. For the larger tank, you will need a strong filter to preserve water quality; for the smaller group, a mature sponge filter should be enough. The tank should be well planted, with a dark substrate and some flat rocks to serve as spawning sites.

Conditioning and Triggers:

Condition together for several weeks with tubifex, daphnia, grindal worms, and brine shrimp. If the male becomes too aggressive during this period, you may need to place a partition in the tank. Raising the temperature by one or two degrees and lowering the pH slightly may trigger spawning.

Spawning: The male displays enthusiastically to the female in a courtship that can last for up to two days. The courting pair then swims circles around one another and "embraces" in typical gourami fashion as the female releases eggs and the male releases sperm. The fertilized eggs will drift to the tank floor or onto a rock, and the female will pick them up in her mouth. Spawning can last up to an hour.

Brood Size: Up to 75.

Fry Care: The fry hatch in their mother's mouth in about six days, but she continues to incubate them for another eight days. During this time, she usually distances herself from tankmates and does not eat. When fry are released, they must be fed almost immediately or they will die; offer baby brine shrimp and microworms three times a day, using an eyedropper to place them in the tank near the fry. Keep the light on in the tank so the fry can find the food. Keep the water level to about 6 inches and aerate gently; cover the tank, since the fry will spend much of their time at the surface. Water quality is critical; change small amounts daily. After about a month, the fry will be large enough to consume most other types of fry food.

Special Notes: This species is extremely difficult to spawn, and it is not uncommon for the eggs to suddenly disappear from the mother's mouth; it may be that they were not fertilized and she spit them out or swallowed them. Fry also have a high mortality rate. For master breeders only!

Catfish

Although the fish in this category belong to different families, they have been grouped together here because they all share a common habitat: the substrate. While many aquarists think of most of them as nothing more than a cleanup crew that can be counted on to keep the tank algae-free and consume bits of flake food that slip past fish higher in the

Many species of Cory Catfishes are easy to spawn in home aquariums.

water column, catfish and other bottom feeders–including such "oddball" species as gobies and eels–are fascinating in their own right. Many are easily bred in home aquaria.

Bronze Cory

Scientific Name: *Corydoras aeneus*

Breeding Strategy: Substrate spawner.

Ease of Breeding: Easy.

Introduction: Natives of South America, Bronze Corys have been bred in captivity since the turn of the last century. They can be spawned in species tanks or in a breeding tank that includes at least two males for every female. Like all *Corydoras* catfishes, they are happiest in groups of at least six.

Sex Differences: Females are larger and thicker than males.

Water Conditions: Not critical.

Equipment: A 15-gallon tank equipped with heater and filter. Substrate should be sand or fine gravel with rounded edges to prevent injury to the fishes' delicate barbells (which, incidentally, are integral to the spawning process). Include plants, such as *Cryptocoryne*, that have broad, stiff leaves.

Conditioning and Triggers: Condition separately on blood worms, tubifex, and white worms. When in spawning condition, the metallic sheen of the male becomes more intense; the female's belly becomes plump and reddish in color. Raising the tank temperature to 80°, then allowing it to fall overnight to 65°F, seems to trigger breeding, as does a large water change with cooler water than that of the tank.

Spawning: There are several stages to spawning. First, the male and female chase each other excitedly around the tank, sometimes for as long as several hours. They then select and clean a series of potential spawning sites, such as the undersides of leaves and the side of the tank itself, something that also may take an hour or two. Finally, the female butts the male's vent with her head, and he clasps her barbells with his pectoral spines. Locked in this *T* position, she releases a small number of eggs, and he releases sperm. The female then clasps the eggs in her ventral fins and rushes to deposit them in one of the prepared sites. She then returns to spawn with the same male or another. After spawning, remove the adults to prevent them from eating the eggs.

Brood Size: Three hundred or more.

Fry Care: Fry hatch in three to four days and become free swimming about five days after that. Feed infusoria, baby brine shrimp, and microworms. Do regular partial water changes, but do *not* siphon out the mulm on the bottom of the tank; the fry hide in this, and experienced breeders report that it is critical to the success of raising these fish.

Bristlenose Catfish

Scientific Name: *Ancistrus* spp.

Breeding Strategy: Cave spawner.

Ease of Breeding: Easy.

Introduction: These catfish are perennially popular, not just for their novel looks but for their industriousness: Within days of adding a bristlenose to a tank, every trace of algae will be gone. These catfish breed fairly easily in community or species tanks.

Sex Differences: Mature males have much longer "bristles" than females, and tend to be larger.

Water Conditions: Although not critical, bristlenose seem to prefer water that is on the acidic side; aim for a pH of between 6.5 and 7.0, and hardness of no more than 10 dH. Temperature should be between 75° and 80°F.

Equipment: A single pair can be bred in a 15-gallon tank, but will also breed in a community tank, with size depending on the needs of the other occupants. Make sure there are plenty of hiding places, such as PVC pipe, flowerpots tipped on their sides, and bogwood, which bristlenose will both eat and hide under. They also appreciate a dense fringe of plants around the perimeter of the tank. Add a filter (either sponge or power), an airstone, and a pump, since bristlenose like well-oxygenated water.

Conditioning and Triggers: Condition on shrimp pellets, and vegetable matter such as parboiled zucchini or cucumber. A large water change sometimes seems to trigger spawning, as does a slight increase in temperature. Some breeders also report these fish spawn more readily in the late autumn.

Spawning: Some bristlenose catfish spend days courting; others get right down to business. The male stakes out a nest site in a flowerpot, coconut cave, or piece of PVC pipe, and the female joins him, laying a clutch of semi-adhesive, amber-colored eggs. After the male fertilizes them, the female departs and the male remains, fanning the eggs with his fins to aerate them.

Brood Size: Fifty or more.

Fry Care: The male guards the nest until the eggs hatch, usually in three to five days. The fry become free swimming within a week after that. Feed crushed vegetables such as blanched lettuce, peas, and zucchini, as well as baby brine shrimp and minced bloodworms. Keep in mind that bristlenose are bottom feeders, so if they spawn in a community tank, it's important to make sure some of the baby brine shrimp make it all the way to the bottom without being snatched up by other fish. You can also put rocks in jars of tank water on a sunny windowsill until they develop a good coating of algae, then put them in the tank for the fry to feed on. Change 10 percent of water daily.

Special Note: Some female *Ancistrus* have been observed laying eggs in the nests of males already guarding fry—possibly because those males have proven their parenting skills. Some scientists theorize that the bristles on the male's nose, which somewhat resemble larval fry, may trick a female into thinking a male is a good parent and mating with him.

"Cuckoo" Catfish

Scientific Name: *Synodontis multipunctatus*

Breeding Strategy: Egg layer.

Ease of Breeding: Moderate.

Introduction: This catfish, which has become of increasing interest to aquarists in recent years, gets its common name from its unusual breeding behavior: It lays its eggs among those of an unwitting host fish—usually a mouthbrooding African cichlid – and leaves them for the host to incubate along with its own. *S. multipunctatus* does not mature sexually until it is between three and five years old.

Sex Differences: Females are larger and plumper. Males have a taller dorsal fin.

Water Conditions: Although these fish can live in a wide range of conditions, for breeding, aim for a pH of between 7.8 and 8.2 and a temperature of 75° to 82°F. Keep up with water changes, since high levels of nitrates stress these fish.

Equipment: Size and setup of tank depends to a large degree on size and needs of host fish. Equip the tank with good filtration and lots of hiding places; these catfish particularly like caves.

Conditioning and Triggers: Condition *S. multipunctatus* on brine shrimp, blood worms, and krill, while simultaneously conditioning the host fish. The courting activities of the host fish trigger *S. multipunctatus* to spawn.

Spawning: When the male catfish senses courting activity on the part of the cichlids, he hustles to round up his own mate, herding her toward the cichlids' spawning site. (This sometimes causes tussles with the male cichlid, who doesn't appreciate the interruption.) Eventually, however, the catfish will successfully dart in, gobble some of the cichlid eggs, and flee. On the next pass, they'll hastily spawn and flee again, leaving about 20 of their own bright green fertilized eggs behind for the female mouthbrooder to incubate. This may be repeated five or more times while the cichlids are spawning.

Brood Size: Up to 100.

Fry Care: The *S. multipunctatus* eggs begin to hatch in about 48 to 72 hours. If the eggs of the host fish do not hatch at the same time, the *S. multipunctatus* fry may begin to eat them. In addition, the spines of the catfish fry can injure the mouth or gills of the host fish. For this reason, many breeders prefer to strip the host fish. If eggs are placed in an incubator, add an airstone to keep water circulating around them gently. Feed fry with baby brine shrimp for the first month; then introduce chopped blood worms, microworms, and other meaty foods. As fry grow, they will take chopped blood worms and ground-up pellets. They require plenty of room if they are to achieve maximum growth rates, so rear them in a tank of at least 30 gallons, with 55 being even better.

Special Notes: These fish are native to Africa's Lake Tanganyika, but interestingly, cichlids from the same lake do not make good hosts, because they seem more able to distinguish the catfish eggs from their own. Instead, many breeders report success using cichlids from other rift lakes, such as mouthbrooders of the genus *Haplochromis.*

False Corydoras

Scientific Name: *Aspidoras paucira-diatus*

Breeding Strategy: Egg layer.

Ease of Breeding: Difficult.

Introduction: Like many species of *Corydoras* catfish, this fish is native to the Amazon Basin of Brazil. It so closely resembles a Cory that when first described in 1970, it was placed in the same genus; later it was reclassified. *A. pauciradiatus* is happiest in groups of

Part 2

six or more. It has been bred in captivity, but infrequently; it is a fish to aspire to once you have mastered all of the techniques necessary to spawn less difficult fish.

Sex Differences: Males are larger and slimmer than females.

Water Conditions: Soft, acidic water, with a pH of about 6.0 and a dH no greater than 12. Temperature should be between 70° and 78°F. These fish also like strong currents and highly oxygenated water.

Equipment: These fish can be bred in species tanks of 20 gallons. Add power filter, air-stone, pump, heater, and a sand substrate. Plant densely, including many clumps of Java moss as spawning sites. Some breeders use a powerhead attached to sponge filter to create horizontal water flow in the tank. A barometer, while not required, can be useful, since some breeders report that the drop in barometric pressure that accompanies storms seems to trigger spawning.

Conditioning and Triggers: Condition together on white worms, black worms, brine shrimp, and other high-protein foods. Females in breeding condition become so full of eggs that they look bloated. When the barometric pressure begins to drop, do a water change of 50 to 75 percent, replacing the tank water with slightly cooler water that is very soft and acidic.

Spawning: There are few descriptions of the actual spawning; it is known to be preceded by frantic swimming, sometimes vertically in the water column. The eggs are laid among dense clumps of plants or on the sides of the tank. There are also a couple of reports of these fish spawning on the filter; some experts theorize that this is linked to the fishes' love of heavily oxygenated, moving water.

Brood Size: Up to 50.

Fry Care: Fry hatch in about four days. When their yolk sacs have been absorbed and they become free swimming, feed microworms, baby brine shrimp, and powdered fry food two or three times a day. Do water changes of 25 percent twice a week.

Characins

The Family Characidae is sometimes referred to as a sort of catchall category, because it comprises such a wide variety of fish. For instance, Neon Tetras are characins–and so are piranhas, hatchetfish, and blind cavefish among many others.

Many–although not all–characins are schooling fish that will happily breed in

Cardinal Tetras will offer advanced hobbyists quite a challenge to spawn in captivity.

species tanks. In general, they also prefer soft and acidic water, dim lighting, and lots of plants.

Lemon Tetra

Scientific Name: *Hyphessobrycon pulchripinnis*

Breeding Method: Egg scatterer.

Ease of Breeding: Moderate.

Introduction: Although they are often over-looked in favor of their Neon and Cardinal cousins, Lemon Tetras have a subtle beauty and peaceful disposition that make them ideal aquarium inhabitants. They can be spawned in pairs or in a species tank of one male to four or five females.

Sex Differences: Females have deeper bodies than males; the anal fin of the males is edged in black.

Water Conditions: Although there are reports of these fish spawning in water with a pH as high as 8.0, they seem happier in soft, acidic water with a pH of somewhere between 6.5 and 7.2; many breeders achieve this by filtering through peat. Temperature should be between 74° and 79°F.

Equipment: Start with a tank of at least 5 gallons for a breeding pair, or 10 gallons for a group. Add a sponge filter, a heater, and a spawning grate, along with some plants or spawning mops and some Java moss if the fry are to be raised in the tank. Cover three sides and the top with dark paper to keep the lighting subdued.

Conditioning and Triggers: Condition separately for a week or two before spawning, feeding live foods such as brine shrimp, blood worms, *Daphnia*, and white worms. Make sure the water quality is pristine.

Spawning: Place the breeding pair or group in the tank in the late afternoon. They will usually spawn the next morning, with the male dancing and displaying vigorously to his chosen mate. He will then lure her to his chosen spawning site, where she will release a few eggs and he will fertilize them. The eggs will drift to the bottom of the tank. The performance may be repeated several times over the course of an hour. If there is no spawning grate to protect the eggs, either they or the parents should be transferred to another tank.

Brood Size: 100 – 200 on average.

Fry Care: Keep the rearing tank covered, as eggs are sensitive to light. They will hatch in about 24 hours; at this point, you can allow some light into the tank. Fry become free swimming about five days after hatching. Feed infusoria; vinegar eels can be added after two or three days, and by the eighth day, fry should be large enough to take baby brine shrimp. Change 10 to 25 percent of water daily until the fry are several months old.

Species with Similar Breeding Habits: Black Widow Tetra *(Gymnocorymbus ternetzi)*; Silvertip Tetra *(Hasemania nana)*; Glowlight Tetra *(Hemigrammus erythrozonus)*; Rummynose tetra *(Hemigrammus bleheri)*; Buenos Aires Tetra *(Hyphessobrycon anisitsi)*; Serpae Tetra *(Hyphessobrycon eques)*; Bleeding-heart Tetra *(Hyphessobrycon erythrostigma)*.

Neon Tetra

Scientific Name: *Paracheirodon innesi*

Breeding Method: Egg scatterer.

Ease of Breeding: Moderate.

Introduction: For years, the only Neons available to hobbyists were wild-caught; today, a better understanding of their spawning habits has made it possible for both commercial fish farms and hobbyists to breed them in captivity.

Sex Differences: Difficult to distinguish, although females in breeding condition tend to be plumper than the males. Many breeders solve the problem of sexing Neons by spawning them in small groups.

Water Conditions: Soft, acidic water, with a pH of 6.0 or lower and hardness between 2 and 3 dH. Some breeders report success using water filtered over peat or adding black-water extract to the tank. Temperature should be about 77°F.

Equipment: A 10-gallon tank, situated in a spot where it will receive only subdued lighting. Cover or paint the back and sides to further cut down on light. Add Java moss or a thin layer of peat to the bottom of the tank as a spawning substrate.

Conditioning and Triggers: Fish become sexually mature around seven or eight months of age. Separately condition males and females (assuming you can tell which is which) for about a week on brine shrimp and tubifex worms. Some breeders report that covering the tank entirely, then gradually uncovering over a period to increase light levels and simulate daybreak, seems to trigger spawning.

Part 2

Spawning: The fish usually begin courting a day or so after being placed in the breeding tank, but may not spawn for several days after that. Males chase the females around wildly; the pair then release eggs and milt above a clump of Java moss or peat on the substrate. The fertilized eggs, no larger than grains of sand, drift down into the moss. Remove the adults to prevent them from eating their eggs, and cover the top of the aquarium with dark paper or cloth, since the eggs are very sensitive to light.

Brood Size: Up to 400.

Fry Care: Fry will hatch in 24 to 36 hours, and become free swimming a few days after that. Feed infusoria or liquid fry food for the first week, then add baby brine shrimp to their diet. At that time, also add a sponge filter. Make sure the fry have plenty to eat, but do not overfeed – they have been known to eat to the point where their stomachs burst. Begin water changes after three weeks, removing very small quantities and replacing them with water of the same parameters. After eight weeks, gradually substitute water that is a little harder and has a pH closer to that in which they'll be living as adults. Neon fry do not begin to take on their adult colors until they are about a half-inch in size.

Species with Similar Breeding Habits: Cardinal Tetra *(Paracheirodon axelrodi)*; Black Neon *(Hyphessobrycon herbertaxelrodi).*

Three-striped Pencilfish

Scientific Name: *Nannostomus eques*

Breeding Strategy: Plant chooser.

Ease of Breeding: Moderate.

Introduction: These peaceful schooling fish are named for their long, thin bodies and pointed noses as well as their unusual behavior: They often swim at a 45 degree angle.

Sex Differences: Males are more brightly colored; females tend to be plumper. Start with a group of six or eight and let them pair off naturally.

Water Conditions: Soft and acidic, with pH of 6.5 or lower and dH of about 5. Temperature should be between 77° and 86°, with the upper end of that range being preferable. Breeders disagree as to whether to add substrate: The fish will be more relaxed with a dark substrate—a covering of waterlogged peat will accomplish this, and has the added benefits of softening the water and staining it a dark color. Alternatively, use blackwater extract to darken and soften the water.

Equipment: Breeding tank of at least 10 gallons, equipped with heater, sponge filter, spawning grate, and broad-leaved plants such as Amazon swordplants or *Cryptocoryne*. Since this will also serve as the rearing tank, do not use substrate; instead, put the plants in pots or weight them to the substrate. Set the tank in a quiet, dimly lit location.

Conditioning and Triggers: Condition males and females separately on mosquito larvae, daphnia, blood worms, and other live foods for one to two weeks prior to spawning.

Spawning: Move the breeding pair to the tank in the late afternoon or early evening. Within a day or two, the male should begin displaying to the female, flaring his fins, and chasing her around the tank; usually this takes place first thing in the morning. Eventually, they will maneuver beneath one of the leaves, where the female will deposit a few eggs at a time and the male will fertilize them. This will be repeated a number of times over the course of one or two hours; some of the eggs will stick to the leaf, but most will drift to the bottom of the tank. Once spawning is complete, the adults should be removed, as they will eat their eggs.

Brood Size: About 30 to 40 on average.

Fry Care: Fry will hatch in 24 to 36 hours and become free swimming five to six days after that. Feed infusoria and green water, introducing baby brine shrimp and microworms as the fry grow. Do daily water changes of 10 to 25 percent to ensure that conditions are top notch, and use a sponge filter. Fry grow slowly, taking nearly a year to reach sexual maturity.

Marbled Hatchetfish

Scientific Name: *Carnegiella strigata*

Breeding Strategy: Egg layer.

Ease of Breeding: Moderate.

Introduction: These unusually-shaped fish are the smallest members of the hatchetfish family, and the easiest to keep and breed in captivity. They are peaceful but are most comfortable in groups of their own species. They can be spawned in a breeding tank or a species tank.

Sex Differences: Difficult to distinguish, although females are often a bit larger than males and plumper when viewed from above. Consider buying a group of juveniles and allowing them to pair off naturally as they mature.

Water Conditions: Although these fish can be maintained in a wide range of water conditions, they are fussy when it comes to spawning, preferring a pH of between 5.5 and 6.5, and a dH of about 5. Keep the lighting subdued, and add peat or blackwater extract to darken the water. Temperature should be between 75° and 84°.

Equipment: These fish can be spawned in a small group in a tank of at least 20 gallons, and preferably larger, placed in a quiet location where it will get filtered sunlight. Add heater and sponge filter. Plant densely around the edges, and add floating plants, which will give fish both a sense of security and potential spawning sites. Make sure the tank is covered, as these fish love to jump.

Conditioning and Triggers: These fish love insects, so condition with plenty of mosquito larvae and fruit flies as well as daphnia, blood worms, and brine shrimp. Raising the temperature a few degrees may trigger spawning.

Spawning: During courtship, the male circles and dashes past the female; they may also make numerous leaps out of the water. The actual spawning takes place in the upper region of the tank, with the pair in a side-by-side, head-to-tail position. The fertilized eggs are released into the floating plants but are not adhesive and will immediately fall to the substrate. Remove the parents after spawning, as they will eat the eggs.

Brood Size: Not available.

Fry Care: The fry hatch in two to three days, and become free swimming five days after that. Feed infusoria or commercial fry food, adding baby brine shrimp a few days later.

Red-bellied Piranha

Scientific Name: *Pygocentrus nattereri*

Breeding Strategy: Nest builder.

Ease of Breeding: Moderate with captive bred specimens, difficult with wild-collected individuals.

Introduction: Despite their fierce reputation, piranhas make fascinating aquarium residents and are generally well mannered as long as their keepers take a few precautions—giving them plenty to eat, and never sticking their bare hands into the tank without knowing where the piranhas are in relation to your fingers! Also, it is important to

know that it is illegal to keep piranhas in some states so be sure to check your local and state regulations before purchasing them. Red-bellied Piranhas are mature enough to breed when they are about 6 inches in size.

Sex Differences: Can be difficult to distinguish, especially in juveniles. Mature males tend to be darker than females, who have a more yellow tinge, but the difference is so subtle that it may not be apparent to an inexperienced eye. Many breeders buy groups of six or eight and let them pair off naturally.

Water Conditions: Hardness and pH not critical, but piranhas like temperatures in the 77° to 80°F range.

Equipment: Piranhas can be bred in a species aquarium, or the pair can be placed in a breeding tank. For the latter, use a tank that is a *minimum* of 50 gallons; 100 gallons would be better. Add a canister or power filter and substrate such as fine gravel for a nest site. Floating plants may help the fish feel more secure.

Conditioning and Triggers: Allow fish to pair off from the school naturally; you will know when they have done so because they will select a territory and begin chasing other fish away; they will also darken in color, becoming a purplish black. Condition on feeder fish and chunks of meat. Some breeders say raising the temperature slightly, to about 82°F, may trigger spawning; others say that lowering the water in the tank, then using fresh water to raise it again gradually, will have the same result.

Spawning: The male will begin shifting gravel around, building a nest, while the female watches. When he is done, he will urge her toward the nesting site, and she will help him to put the final touches on it. When ready to spawn, they will circle each other, then begin swimming side by side. Heads pointing toward the substrate, they begin to release eggs and sperm, sometimes nipping and slapping at each other with their tails. The process is repeated numerous times until all eggs have been released, something that can take hours. Afterward the male usually guards the eggs, fiercely protecting them from tankmates who get too close. It is not necessary to remove the female.

Brood Size: Between 500 and 1,500.

Fry Care: The male will fan his fins to keep oxygenated water circulating over the orangey-colored eggs, which will hatch in about two days and become free swimming about a week later. It is best to remove fry to a separate tank (a 20-gallon tank will be large enough at first) either before they hatch or immediately afterward. Keep water circulating with a pump and airstone. Feed with baby brine shrimp; later you can add ground cichlid pellets, blood worms, and commercial fry food.

Silver Dollars

Scientific Name: *Metynnis* spp.

Breeding Method: Egg scatterer.

Ease of Breeding: Moderate.

Introduction: Native to South America, these large, peaceful fish—named for their round, silver bodies—make good community-tank inhabitants. They can be spawned in pairs in a breeding tank, or collectively in a species tank, as long as it is large enough.

Sex Differences: The male's anal fin is reddish and rounder than that of the female; the female's fins are colorless.

Water Conditions: Hardness and pH do not appear to be critical, although in the wild,

these fish live in soft, acidic water. Filtering over peat or adding blackwater extract will help to accomplish this, while staining the water brown is something that these fish appreciate. Temperature should be between 75° and 82°F, with the upper end of that range being preferable.

Equipment: Start with a breeding tank of at least 30 gallons for a pair, or 55 or larger for a school. Place in a quiet location with sub-dued lighting and add heater, filter, bog-wood, and lots of plants. If the parents are to remain in the tank, a spawning grate will prevent them from eating their eggs.

Conditioning and Triggers: Condition the sexes together or separately. These fish are largely herbivorous, so include plenty of vegetables such as lettuce, spinach, and blanched peas that have been squeezed from their shell; many will also take brine shrimp and other live foods, although these should not make up the bulk of their diet.

Spawning: The male chases the female around the tank, nudging her abdomen. When ready to spawn, they repeatedly press their bodies together, with the male sometimes bending around the female. This often takes place in or around plants; some aquarists report that their Silver Dollars have spawned in the roots of floating plants. The two quiver as eggs and sperm are released; the fertilized eggs then drift to the substrate.

Brood Size: Varies widely, from about 300 to more than 1,500.

Fry Care: The fry hatch in about two days, and become free swimming within a week. At this time, begin to feed infusoria and brine shrimp. By the end of a month, fry will be big enough to eat flake food ground into a powder. Be sure to include lots of vegetable matter.

Blind Cave Tetra

Scientific Name: *Astyanax* sp. aff. *mexicanus*

Breeding Method: Egg scatterer.

Ease of Breeding: Moderate.

Introduction: Blind Cave Fish are native to the inky waters of caves in Mexico and Central America, where vision would provide no benefit. Although they are born with eyes, these gradually disappear as the fish mature, and adults navigate using their lateral line, tracking down food by smell. Blind cave fish can be bred as a pair or in a species tank, but unlike many other tetras, do not school.

Sex Differences: Can be difficult to distinguish. When in breeding condition, females are plumper than males.

Water Conditions: Hardness and pH do not appear to be critical, although blind cave fish may spawn a bit more readily in soft, acidic water. This fish also tolerates a wide range of temperatures, but appears more likely to spawn in water that is between 66° and 70°F.

Equipment: Tank should be 10 gallons for a breeding pair, 20 gallons for a small group. Add plenty of plants, a heater, and a sponge filter.

Conditioning and Triggers: Condition for at least a week on live foods such as brine shrimp and *Daphnia*. Decreasing the temperature a degree or two may trigger spawning.

Spawning: These fish don't seem to do much courting – perhaps because displaying to one another would have no point. The females simply lay their eggs and the males fertilize them. The eggs then drift to the substrate.

Brood Size: About 100.

Fry Size: The fry hatch in 24 to 72 hours, and become free swimming about a week later. Feed baby brine shrimp, microworms, and other small fish.

Special Notes: These fish can crossbreed with the sighted *Astyanax fasciatus,* and should not be kept in the same tank.

Cichlids

There are an estimated 1,500 fish in the Family Cichlidae, including angelfish, one of the most recognizable and popular fish in captivity. Because there are so many species of cichlids hailing from so many different habits—from the rocky rift lakes of Africa to the rivers of South America—it is difficult to generalize about them. Cichlids can be substrate spawners, nest

Cichlids are known for their advanced and dedicated brood care.

builders, mouthbrooders, or cave spawners, and their tank setup should depend on their breeding strategy.

Angelfish

Scientific Name: *Pterophyllum scalare*

Breeding Method: Substrate chooser.

Ease of Breeding: Moderate.

Introduction: With their triangular bodies and long flowing fins, angelfish are arguably the most recognizable of all aquarium fish. They are easy to keep and come in many color morphs.

Sex Differences: Can be difficult to distinguish. Mature females have a slight bulge in the belly area when viewed head on; males tend to be larger and their heads are slightly more curved. The male's breeding tube is pointed, while the female's is rounded, but this is evident only during spawning. Many breeders buy

Target Fish

Sometimes, fish are reluctant to spawn no matter how perfect their setup. If they're a territorial species, as is the case with many cichlids, they can sometimes be prodded into breeding by the proximity of a *target fish*—a fish the male perceives as competition, which serves to strengthen his bond with his mate.

It's usually best when the target fish and breeding pair are of the same or closely related species. Some breeders suggest protecting the target fish by separating it from the breeding pair with a glass tank divider; being able to see the target fish is usually enough to get the breeding pair to react.

Target fish are sometimes incorrectly called *dither fish*. In fact, the latter are usually used to give skittish fish confidence; seeing the dither fish swimming openly convinces them there are no predators present and that it is safe to come out of hiding.

a group of juveniles and let them pair off naturally.

Water Conditions: Angelfish prefer soft, acidic water. Aim for a pH of 6.5 or below, and hardness of about 5 dH. Temperature should be between 80° and 84°F.

Equipment: Experienced breeders recommend at *least* a 20-gallon high tank with hood; 30 gallons is even better. Add driftwood and plastic plants to help the angels feel secure, but keep the bottom bare. Prop two or three pieces of slate or slabs of acrylic against the inside tank walls as spawning site. Cover the heater with mesh cover to prevent the angels from laying eggs on it. (Females will attempt to spawn on any vertical surface; there have even been reports of females attempting to lay eggs on their mate's side!) Add a pre-conditioned sponge filter.

Conditioning and Triggers: Condition the breeding pair together in the spawning tank, feeding live foods such as brine shrimp and blood worms. Change at least 50 percent of water weekly; some breeders recommend up to 40 percent a day. Raising the temperature a degree or two or changing up to 75 percent of the water may prod a reluctant pair to spawn.

Spawning: When spawning is imminent, the angels become extremely territorial, selecting and cleaning a spawning site while chasing other fish away. At this point, remove other fish from the tank to protect them and allow the breeding pair to spawn without disturbance. Spawning often takes place during the evening, with the female swimming over the site, her belly almost touching it as she lays rows of adhesive amber-colored eggs. The male swims behind her, fertilizing them. When spawning is complete, the parents will fan water over the eggs with their fins.

Brood Size: Up to 500, with 200 to 300 being more common.

Fry Care: Eggs can be left with their parents, although there is a chance they will be eaten, particularly if it is the breeding pair's first spawn. Alternatively, remove the parents and add an airstone to the tank to keep water circulating around the eggs, or transfer the spawning slate and eggs to a separate tank for incubation. If the latter, add one drop of methylene blue per liter of water as a fungicide, as well as an airstone. Eggs will hatch in one to two days depending on the temperature of the water; the fry are free swimming four to five days after that. Feed them with microworms, baby brine shrimp, or hard-boiled egg yolk squeezed through gauze. Replace half the water each week.

Benga Yellow Peacock

Scientific Name: *Aulonocara baenschi*

Breeding Strategy: Mouthbrooder.

Ease of Breeding: Easy.

Introduction: These spectacular fish from Lake Malawi are peaceful compared to many cichlids, but become aggressive and territorial during spawning.

Sex Differences: Males have bright yellow bodies, and depending on color morph (of which there are several), varying amounts of blue on their heads, bodies, and tails. Females are grayish brown.

Water Conditions: Hard, alkaline water, with a pH of 7.8 to 8.2 and dH of at least 10.

Part 2

Temperature should be between 77° and 82°F.

Equipment: These fish will spawn in a species or community tank of at least 40 gallons, but there should be several females for every male, since males can be aggressive. Add heater, power filter, and fine gravel or sand substrate, since peacocks like to dig, and rock caves to provide hiding places for females (and eventually fry). Plants can also provide shelter, and are rarely bothered by this species.

Conditioning and Triggers: Remove the male from the tank during conditioning, leaving the females. Feed mosquito larvae, brine shrimp, and bloodworms until the females are plump with eggs.

Spawning: After two or three weeks, place the male back in the tank. He should soon begin to court his chosen female, extending his fins and parading in front of her as his colors brighten. The female releases eggs and picks them up immediately; the male fertilizes them by releasing sperm into her mouth. The male should be removed after spawning, as he will often harass the female.

Brood Size: Up to 40.

Fry Care: The mother will spit out the fry after 18 to 20 days. Feed baby brine shrimp, fry food, and crushed flakes.

Special Notes: Females will sometimes swallow the eggs or fry; usually after several spawnings, they become more proficient and are able to successfully raise a brood. Do not keep with other species of peacocks, as they will interbreed.

Species with Similar Breeding Habits: Most of the nearly two dozen species of *Aulonocara*, including the firebird peacock *(A. hansbaenschi);* blue gold peacock *(A. korneliae);* sulfur crest peacock *(A. maylandi);* Grant's peacock *(A. stuartgranti);* blue orchid peacock *(A. kandeensis).*

Cockatoo Dwarf Cichlid

Scientific Name: *Apistogramma cacatuoides*

Breeding Method: Cave spawner.

Ease of Breeding: Easy.

Introduction: These South American cichlids are named for the spectacular crest formed by their dorsal fins. They can be bred in pairs or in a species tank.

Sex Differences: Males are more colorful, and the rays of their dorsal fins are longer.

Water Conditions: Not critical; while many breeders use soft, acidic water, there are reports of cockatoo cichlids spawning in water as high as 7.8; hatches may be smaller in very alkaline water, however. Temperatures should be around 76°F; lower temperatures result in a higher percentage of females, and higher temperatures result in more males.

Equipment: Use a 10-gallon tank for a breeding pair, or a 20-gallon long

tank for one male and five or six females. Some breeders add a layer of gravel, but others prefer to leave the tank bottom bare. Add a heater, a sponge filter, and a number of upturned flowerpots or half coconut shells with "doors" drilled into the sides; also add plenty of plants (in pots if you are not using substrate). Java moss is a good choice, since it will give fry places to hide.

Conditioning and Triggers: Condition the sexes together or separately on live foods such as brine shrimp, blood worms, and tubifex for a week or two before spawning.

Spawning: The colors of both males and females grow more vivid when they are in condition to spawn. A female stakes out one of the "caves" in the tank as her territory; the male shimmies and display his fins to her. When ready to spawn, she flips on her side and turns her belly toward him, pressing close to the spawning surface as she releases her eggs. When spawning is completed, she will drive the male out of the cave and guard the eggs. Some breeders recommend removing the male at this point, because his presence may stress her, but others say that the process of removing him is equally stressful and may cause her to eat her eggs.

Brood Size: Up to 80.

Fry Care: Eggs will hatch in about three days, and become free swimming about a week after that. At this point, expect the mother to reappear with babies in tow. Feed fry three times a day with infusoria and live brine shrimp, introducing other small foods as the fry grow.

Convict Cichlid

Scientific Name: *Archocentrus nigrofasciatus*

Breeding Strategy: Cave breeder.

Ease of Breeding: Easy.

Introduction: Convicts are tough little fish who seem to get equal joy out of tearing up tankmates and tank décor. They are prolific breeders and especially aggressive when spawning, so plan to either put them in a breeding tank or remove everybody else for their own safety.

Sex Differences: Mature males have a bump on their head and dorsal fins that are longer and more pointed; they also tend to be larger than females, who have an orange cast to their bellies and fins.

Water Conditions: Hardness and pH not critical; this fish also tolerates temperatures from 68° to 77°F.

Equipment: Start with a tank of at least 29 gallons; add heater, filter, and rockwork and caves to provide both spawning sites and hiding places for the female and fry.

Conditioning and Triggers: Condition together or separately on live foods such as brine shrimp, tubifex, and blood worms; also add vegetable material such as blanched shelled peas or zucchini. Raising the temperature a few degrees often triggers spawning.

Spawning: The pair display to one another, shaking their heads and dancing. When ready to spawn, they will disappear into their chosen cave, where eggs will be deposited.

Brood Size: Over 200.

Fry Care: Fry hatch in a week and become free swimming three to four days after that. At that point, begin feeding microworms and baby brine shrimp; add other fry foods and flake foods as the fry grow. Despite their aggressiveness toward other fish, convict cichlids make excellent parents, driving off tankmates that venture too close. There are even reports of convicts hiding their young in the substrate to protect them from perceived predators.

Discus

Scientific Name: *Symphysodon aequifasciatus* and *S. discus*

Breeding Method: Nest builders.

Ease of Breeding: Moderate to Difficult.

Introduction: These fish are often called "the king of aquarium fish," and with good reason: their saucer-shaped bodies, languid swimming patterns, and bright colors

Part 2

make them a standout in any tank. However, they are finicky about the parameters of the water in which they are maintained, and even fussier when breeding.

Sex Differences: Difficult to distinguish. Males' spawning tubes are thin and pointy, while females' are wider and blunt-edged, but since the tubes are visible only when spawning is imminent, many breeders start with a group of a half dozen juveniles and allow them to pair off naturally.

Water Conditions: Discus require very soft, acidic water in order to breed. Aim for a pH of about 6.5, and a dH of about 2 or 3. Temperature should be 82° to 86°F.

Equipment: Start with a tank of at least 50 gallons and a mature filter, located in a quiet area away from direct sun. For ease of cleaning, keep the bottom substrate free, but add potted plants to help the discus feel more secure. Add spawning slates propped at an angle against the side of the tank or some commercially available terracotta spawning cones. Discus may attempt to spawn on the heater, so cover it with mesh to protect the eggs.

Conditioning and Triggers: Breeders report success raising a group of Discus in the main tank, then removing all but the breeding pair so as not to stress the bond between them. Condition Discus on beef heart and freeze-dried and live foods, and change about 20 percent of the water daily to prevent pH swings from decomposing food. Reluctant pairs may be convinced to spawn by raising or lowering the temperature slightly, or doing a large water change using water very slightly cooler than that in the tank.

Spawning: Spawning often takes place in the evening. The pair will begin to clean their chosen site—usually a spawning slate, but sometimes one of the leaves of a plant. They may also "shimmy" at one another, and their colors may become brighter. Then the female will lay a string of eggs on the nesting site and the male will fertilize them; when spawning is completed, they will take turns guarding the eggs.

Brood Size: Up to 400.

Fry Care: The fry hatch in anywhere from 24 to 60 hours, and become free swimming in about five days. For ten days after that, they will feed off their parents' slime coats, although they may also accept baby brine shrimp during this time. You may notice the parents bickering as they attempt to pass the fry off on one another. If this occurs, separate them with a tank divider that has perforations large enough to allow the fry to move through. Water quality is critical when rearing dis-

cus fry; do small partial water changes on a daily basis.

Special Notes: Discus do not sexually mature until they are at least two years old.

Kribensis

Scientific Name: *Pelvicachromis pulcher*

Breeding Strategy: Cave spawner.

Ease of Breeding: Moderate.

Introduction: Kribensis—or "kribs" for short—are among the most popular of South American cichlids, and are excellent parents; their spawning and fry-care behaviors are fascinating to watch.

Sex Differences: Males have pointed tail and dorsal fins, while those of females are more rounded. Females are usually smaller and more colorful than males.

Water Conditions: Temperature should be between 72° and 82°F, with a pH of 7.0 to 7.4. According to some breeders, an alkaline pH produces mostly male offspring, while an acid pH produces mostly females. (Neutral water produces roughly even numbers of both.)

Equipment: A breeding tank of at least 20 gallons, and preferably larger. Add heater, a substrate of sand or fine gravel, and a power filter. For spawning sites, include clay pots, rocks glued into cave formations with aquarium-grade silicone, or sections of PVC pipe. (You can also use half a coconut shell, scraped clean and boiled for 30 minutes.)

Conditioning and Triggers: Condition together, as these fish form strong pair bonds. A large water change—50 to 75 percent of the tank water—will often trigger spawning. The presence of a target fish may help to strengthen their bond and induce them to spawn.

Spawning: The female flirts with the male, showing her belly and shimmying in front of him. If he is agreeable, they will select a cave in which to spawn and move the gravel around inside until the arrangement meets their satisfaction. Then the female will deposit the eggs on the cave ceiling and the male will fertilize them. The female will guard the eggs, and the male will guard her. If there are other fish in the tank (which is not recommended), he will drive them away ferociously.

Brood Size: 50 to 100.

Fry Care: The eggs hatch in three to eight days, and fry are free swimming about a week after that. Feed several times a day with baby brine shrimp, fry food, and/or flakes crushed to a powder, but keep an eye on water quality and do frequent small changes, since krib fry are sensitive. You should also keep an eye on the parents; if they become too aggressive with one another, remove one.

Special Notes: Before the babies become free swimming, krib parents sometimes move them around in their mouths; afterward, they sometimes herd them into a school and escort them around the tank.

Oscar

Scientific Name: *Astronotus* spp.

Breeding Method: Substrate spawner.

Ease of Breeding: Difficult.

Introduction: Many aquarists consider Oscars to be among the smartest—if not *the* smartest—fish kept in home aquaria. Oscars seem to recognize the person who feeds them, and grow very tame, eating from their owner's hand and sometimes even surfacing to get their backs scratched. The drawback is that they grow very large, so steer clear of this fish if you don't have a lot of tank space.

Sex Differences: Can be difficult to distinguish without comparing the fishes' vent areas. Some aquarists insist males have slightly larger and pointier dorsal fins and slightly redder sides, and that overall, females are smaller than males. The male's breeding tube is narrower and more pointed than the female's, but this is visible only when spawning is imminent.

Water Conditions: Hardness and pH not critical. Temperature should be between 75° and 80°F.

Equipment: Minimum tank size for a breeding pair is 55 gallons; a tank twice that large would be even better. Equip with filter, heater, and some large flat rocks that can serve both as spawning sites and shields for the female if the male becomes too aggressive. Gravel is optional, although Oscars do enjoy pushing it around the tank! Some breeders recommend covering the sides of the tank with paper so as not to disturb the fish; if you want to watch them courting, cut a peephole.

Conditioning and Triggers: Condition separately for a week or two on feeder

fish, earthworms, blood worms, shrimp and/or crayfish, and other live food. Gradually raising the temperature to 84° or 86°F may trigger breeding, as will doing a large water change.

Spawning: Courtship behavior is sometimes hard to distinguish from aggression; the fish slap each other with their tails and lock lips in what is believed to be a test of strength. (If one of the fish is clearly beating up the other, separate them.) Sometimes courting Oscars open their mouths in unison as if they are yawning. Eventually, they will select a spawning site and meticulously clean it. Then the female lays her eggs in rows on the rock and the male fertilizes them. Afterward, both parents will fan the eggs with their fins to keep oxygenated water circulating around them. They may also mouth the eggs, destroying those that have not been fertilized and are at risk of fungus. Although both parents usually share guarding duties, there are reports of the male becoming aggressive and trying to take over entirely; if this occurs, remove the female for her own safety.

Brood Size: As many as 1,500.

Fry Care: Fry hatch in two to three days, and become free swimming about four days after that. Feed baby brine shrimp for the first week or so; then add daphnia and chopped tubifex. Oscar fry can also eat crushed flake food, but that should not make up the bulk of their diet. Some breeders recommend shutting off the filter during feeding, to make it easier for the fry to locate and catch the food. Some Oscars eat their fry once they become free swimming; you may wish to remove them at that point to protect the fry.

Zebra Mbuna

Scientific Name: *Metriaclima zebra* (formerly *Pseudotropheus zebra*)

Breeding Method: Mouthbrooder.

Ease of Breeding: Moderate.

Introduction: This cichlid, one of the first mbuna in the trade, comes in many color morphs, including electric blue, red, orange, and gold. There is also an albino strain. They are extremely easy to spawn, and will do so in any tank set up for Malawi cichlids. However, they readily crossbreed with other species, so it is best to keep and breed them only in species or spawning setups that include one male and at least two females.

Sex Differences: Males are much more

colorful than females, and also have large round dots on their anal fins.

Water Conditions: Hard and alkaline, with a dH of 10 to 20 and a pH of between 7.5 and 8.5; fish kept in the higher pH often yield more fry. Temperature should be in the mid-70s. Mbuna like clean water, so keep up with water changes.

Equipment: Tank should be a minimum of 30 gallons, but bigger would be even better, since these fish are aggressive and the females need room to get away from the males. Furnish with heater, filter, and plenty of rockwork and PVC pipe to provide hiding places for both females and fry.

Conditioning and Triggers: Mbuna are primarily herbivores, so conditioning should include plenty of vegetable matter, such as *Spirulina*, lettuce, peas, and cucumbers. (Some breeders recommend avoiding live food, particularly blood worms, which are associated with the potentially lethal problem known as Malawi bloat.) A massive water change will sometimes trigger spawning.

Spawning: The male stakes out a territory, and when a female is ready to spawn, she approaches. He shakes and displays and the two circle one another; they may act aggressively. When ready, the female lays a few eggs and then picks them up in her mouth. The male displays his anal fins, which are covered with distinctive marking called "egg spots" because they so closely resemble roe that even the female is fooled by them. She prods the spots, trying to pick them up; scientists theorize that this stimulates the male to release sperm, fertilizing the eggs already in her mouth. This process may be repeated numerous times over the course of an hour or so. When spawning is complete, it is best to transfer the female to a tank of her own, so she can incubate the fry in peace.

Brood Size: Up to 50, although smaller broods are more common.

Fry Care: The female incubates the fry until they are free swimming, three to four weeks after spawning. At this time, remove the mother to a tank of her own and feed her well, as she will be emaciated and weak from going nearly a month without eating. Feed fry on baby brine shrimp and microworms until they are at least an inch in size. By the time they're a month old, you can also feed pulverized flake food formulated for herbivores.

Species with Similar Breeding Habits: Most mbuna, including *Iodotropheus sprengerae; Labeotropheus trewavasae; Labeotropheus fuelleborni; Labidochromis caeruleus; Melanochromis auratus;* and *Melanochromis johannii.*

Many-Banded Shell Dweller

Scientific Name: *Neolamprologus multifasciatus*

Breeding Method: Shell spawner.

Ease of Breeding: Moderate.

Introduction: "Multis," as they are sometimes called, are native to Africa's Lake Tanganyika, and are the smallest known cichlid. In fact, they are sometimes referred to

as a "desktop cichlids" because they don't mind living in very small tanks. It is best to spawn them in a species tank (or a community tank that does not include other bottom dwellers) with a ratio of three or four females to every male.

Sex Differences: Adult males are noticeably larger than females.

Water Conditions: Hard and alkaline, with a pH above 7.8 and a dH of 10 to 20. Temperature should be between 78° and 80°F.

Equipment: A 10-gallon tank with heater and sponge filter. Add a sand substrate—these fish love to dig—and at least two shells (preferably three) for every fish in the tank. Some aquarists report success using "elbows" of PVC pipe instead of shells. Plastic plants are optional; live ones rarely survive the tendency of these fish to continuously rearrange the tank décor.

Conditioning and Triggers: Condition on brine shrimp, vegetable flakes, and blood worms. Removing 50 percent of the water and replacing it with water that is several degrees warmer than that of the tank sometimes triggers spawning.

Spawning: The male and female posture to one another, remaining perfectly still in the water with fins outstretched. Then they alternate going in and out of one of the shells, where the female lays her eggs and the male fertilizes them. Afterward, the female will stay very close to her shell, while the male guards the larger territory.

Brood Size: Up to 30, but smaller broods are common.

Fry Care: The fry hatch in a week to 10 days, but remain so close to the shell for another week or two afterward that they sometimes go unnoticed. Feed infusoria and baby brine shrimp.

Special Notes: Males sometimes bury unused shells in the substrate.

Species with Similar Breeding Habits: *Neolamprologus ocellatus; N. calliurum; N. meleagris.*

Part 2

Cyprinids

Cyprinids are members of the largest family of fish, Cyprinidae, which encompasses more than 2,000 species. Many–from the inch-long Dwarf Rasboras to 3-foot-plus Koi–are kept and bred in captivity.

Because the members of this family are so diverse, it is difficult to generalize about how to breed them. Some,

Tiger Barbs are just one species of barbs that are readily kept and spawned by hobbyists.

such as Zebra Danios, are unfussy and will happily spawn in community or species aquariums. Others, such as Cherry Barbs, are not difficult to spawn, but their fry can be difficult to raise. And still others, such as many species of rasboras, are both difficult to breed and to raise because they require extreme and highly specific water conditions.

In other words, no matter what your skill as a breeder, there is a cyprinid that's right for you!

Cherry Barb

Scientific Name: *Puntius titteya*

Breeding Method: Plant spawner.

Ease of Breeding: Easy to breed, but fry are harder to raise.

Introduction: These fish are among the most popular barbs in the hobby. They tend to be a bit shy, even with members of their own species, and while some breeders report success spawning them in groups, it is more common to breed them in pairs.

Sex Differences: Females are brown, while males are red, especially when in spawning condition.

Water Conditions: Hardness and pH not critical. Temperature 73° to 80°F.

Equipment: Start with a 10- to 20-gallon tank with a tight-fitting cover—during spawning, cherry barbs sometimes become so frenzied that they actually jump out of the tank. Add numerous bushy plants such as *Myriophyllum* or Java moss to serve as spawning sites as well as cover for the female if the male becomes too aggressive.

Conditioning and Triggers: Condition males and females separately with live, frozen, or freeze-dried foods until the females grow plump with eggs. Transfer one or two of the females to the spawning tank in the afternoon; in the evening, add a male. Raising the temperature three or four degrees can sometimes prompt reluctant cherry barbs to spawn.

Spawning: By morning, the male will likely be a deep red, and begin chasing the female around the tank, flaring his fins and "dancing" in front of her as he lures her into the plants. There, they'll turn onto their sides or upside down, and he'll wrap his fins around her body as she releases eggs and he releases milt. Only a few eggs are released at a time, so the spawning process often goes on for several hours. When the pair seems to lose interest in one another, remove them or they will eat the eggs.

Brood Size: About 300.

Fry Care: Within 24 to 48 hours, you will see miniscule fry clinging to the sides of the tank. They will become free swimming in about 36 hours; feed them infusoria and hard-boiled egg yolk squeezed through a clean cloth. Add gentle aeration to circulate the water, and change about 20 percent per day. As fry grow, you can add newly hatched brine shrimp, chopped tubifex worms, and crushed flake food; you should also add a sponge filter.

Tiger Barb

Scientific Name: *Puntius tetrazona*

Breeding Method: Plant spawner.

Ease of Breeding: Easy.

Introduction: Tiger barbs are popular aquarium fish because of their striking appearance. While the most common variety has the black and gold stripes for which they are named, there are a number of other color varieties available, including green, albino, and blushing tiger barbs. These barbs can be nippy, a problem usually alleviated by keeping them in large groups.

Sex Differences: Males are more brightly colored, and the red on their dorsal fins is more intense; in breeding condition, they also develop a red nose. Females tend to be bigger and wider and their noses remain yellowish during spawning.

Water Conditions: Tiger barbs tolerate a wide range of water conditions, but spawn most readily in soft water with a pH of around 6.5 and the temperature set at about 77°F.

Equipment: Breeding tank should be at

least 20 gallons, with a spawning grate or double layer of marbles on the bottom to catch and protect the eggs. Add a mature sponge filter, heater, and plants (artificial plants are okay) or spawning mops.

Conditioning and Triggers: Condition separately on brine shrimp and other live or frozen foods for a week or two before spawning. Sometimes, doing a water change and lowering the depth of the water will trigger a reluctant pair to spawn, as will increasing the temperature a degree or two.

Spawning: Condition the female in the breeding tank or place her in it at least two days before the male. Add the male in the afternoon. The two will soon begin swimming around one another, and the male will display by spreading his fins and hovering head down in the water. Spawning usually takes place the next morning, with the male chasing the female around the tank, nipping at her fins. As they brush up against the plants, she will release several eggs at a time, and the male will fertilize them. The eggs will then drift into the plants and into the crevices between the marbles on the tank bottom. When the female has released all her eggs, the pair will lose interest in one another and should be removed from the tank.

Brood Size: Up to 700.

Fry Care: The eggs will hatch in about two days, and the fry—resembling slivers of glass with eyes—will cling to plants and the sides of the tank. Now is the time to begin culturing infusoria and baby brine shrimp, so when they become free swimming and ready to eat (something that will take about five days), you will be prepared. Feed fry about three times a day, but monitor water quality carefully to make sure it is not being polluted by leftover food. When fry grow larger, you can feed them crushed flakes and daphnia about three times a day.

Species with Similar Breeding Habits: Rosy barb *(Puntius conchonius);* black ruby barb *(P. nigrofasciatus);* checkered barb *(P. oligolepis).*

Zebra Danio

Scientific Name: *Brachydanio rerio*

Breeding Method: Egg scatterer.

Ease of Breeding: Easy.

Introduction: These perennially popular fish are named for the stripes that run the length of their bodies. They are happiest in groups, and zoom around the tank in a blur of activity. They can be bred in community, species, or breeding setups.

Sex Differences: Males have blue and gold stripes, while females have blue and silver stripes, but you'll have to look closely to see the difference. Females also tend to be larger and plumper than males, especially when conditioned for breeding.

Water Conditions: Hardness and pH not critical. Temperature should be between 73° and 79°F.

Equipment: Breeding tank should be at least 24 inches long, since zebra danios like a lot of room to swim. Add heater and filter, plus a spawning grate or substrate of marbles or coarse gravel to protect fry from egg-eating parents.

Conditioning and Triggers: For the highest yield of fry, condition separately for a week to 10 days, feeding live foods four to five times a day. When the female becomes ripe with eggs, transfer the breeding pair – or two males and one female, if you prefer – to the tank you've prepared. You may want to do this late in the evening, since spawning typically occurs at daybreak; some breeders like to position the tank where it receives early-morning sun to encourage this.

Spawning: The male chases the female around the tank. Then he curls around her and releases a cloud of sperm, while the female simultaneously releases a batch of large, clear eggs. The parents may continue to spawn at regular intervals, while the fertilized eggs drift to the bottom of the tank. If there is no spawning grate in the tank, remove the parents after breeding or they may eat the eggs.

Brood Size: Up to 400.

Fry Care: Zebra fry hatch between one and four days after spawning, and are free swimming within a week. Feed them infusoria and fry food for the first week; by the second, they should be big enough for baby brine shrimp. In week three, add a sponge filter. They will mature in four to six months.

Special Notes: The eggs produced during a female's first mating may not hatch, but successive spawns should be more fertile.

Goldfish

Scientific Name: *Carassius auratus*

Breeding Method: Egg scatterer.

Ease of Breeding: Easy.

Introduction: Goldfish have been kept in captivity for thousands of years, and are easily bred both indoors and out. They come in many colors and varieties, from egg-shaped orandas to long, lean comets and bubble-eyed celestials. Goldfish prefer cool water and

should not be kept in the same tank as tropical species.

Sex Differences: Males typically have pin-sized bumps called tubercles on their gill plates, which turn white when the fish is in breeding mode. Females are usually plumper than males.

Water Conditions: Not critical as long as neither pH nor hardness is extreme and temperature falls somewhere between 60° and 75°F.

Equipment: A spawning tank of at least 30 gallons, preferably long and low to maximize surface area, filled with 6 to 9 inches of water. Temperature should be between 66° and 74°F. Add a half dozen spawning mops and some plants. As fry grow, you'll need one or more 20-gallon long grow-out tanks equipped with sponge filters and heaters.

Conditioning and Triggers: Start with a single pair or a trio consisting of two males and a female who are at least 18 months old. Condition with plenty of frozen or live foods, such as blood worms, brine shrimp, and earthworms. Change about 20 percent of the water a day. Some pairs spawn almost immediately; others take weeks or months. Dropping the water temperature a few degrees overnight, then raising it first thing in the morning, sometimes prompts spawning. Thunderstorms also sometimes trigger spawning.

Spawning: Usually takes place first thing in the morning. The male chases the female, bumping her abdomen and driving her into the spawning mops; a process that may go on for several hours before she releases her eggs. He follows, fertilizing them. Remove the parents when spawning is complete so they don't eat the eggs.

Brood Size: Up to 2,000.

Fry Care: Fertilized eggs turn yellow or amber within a day. Remove any that remain white or grow fungus. (Some breeders add a few drops of methylene blue to prevent fungus.) Fry hatch within a week, depending on water temperature, and become free swimming two or three days after that. Feed three or four times a day with green water or hard-boiled egg yolk and brine shrimp. Do daily water changes, preferably after feeding, to maintain water quality. Fry need plenty of room to grow properly; at ten days of age, 100 fry can be kept in a tank with a surface area of 144 square inches, but at a month, the same tank should contain no more than 30 fry. Some breeders say fry develop best when temperature is a constant 68°F.

Special Notes: Getting fish in condition to spawn is the hardest part of breeding gold-fish, since in nature they go through a winter dormancy period, then spawn as the water warms up. While this isn't exactly recommended, some breeders have mimicked this by cooling their fish down gradually in the refrigerator, then allowing them to warm back up!

White Cloud Mountain Minnow

Scientific Name: *Tanichthys albonubes*

Breeding Method: Egg layers.

Ease of Breeding: Easy.

Introduction: These active and attractive red-tailed minnows were discovered in a mountain stream in the 1930s by a Chinese Boy Scout. They are hardy and easy to keep in a community tank, although they like lower temperatures than many tropical species. White Clouds are happiest when kept with other members of their own species. They can be bred in community, species, and spawning tanks.

Sex Differences: Males have brighter coloration; females are larger and plumper, particularly when full of eggs.

Water Conditions: Hardness and pH not critical. Temperature should be between 62° and 75°F; if it gets much higher than that, the fish may become stressed.

Equipment: Start with a tank of at least 10 gallons, located where it will get some sun. Add gravel, water, and some fine-leaved plants such as *Fontinalis*, *Myriophyllum,* or *Elodea,* and/or several spawning mops. You should also start an infusoria culture at the time of spawning, since the fry are too tiny to eat most other foods.

Conditioning and Triggers: Start with a pair that is about a year old; some breeders recommend a group of two males and four females. Condition them separately for about a week with live and freeze-dried foods such as brine shrimp and daphnia before moving them to the spawning tank. Some breeders say that leaving the light on for about 14 hours and doing 20-percent water changes every few days also helps bring fish into breeding condition.

Spawning: The male will "dance" in front of the female with his fins spread wide. He may nudge her abdomen. She will choose a plant as a spawning site, and he'll wrap himself around her. She will release her eggs singly. Spawning may continue for several hours. There is disagreement as to whether parents eat their eggs or fry, so keep a close watch and be prepared to remove them if necessary. Lowering the water temperature slightly can sometimes trigger spawning.

Brood Size: Reports vary from three dozen to 300 eggs from a single spawning.

Fry Care: Within 24 to 36 hours, the eggs will hatch and you'll see fry clinging to the sides of the glass. They will use up their yolk sacs and become free swimming within several days. They are too small for most fry foods, so feed infusoria or prepared fry food. Within a few days, you can add microworms, and after about a week, newly hatched brine shrimp. The fry are sensitive to both water quality and fluctuating water conditions, so do small regular changes and be sure to keep the temperature stable.

Special Notes: Fry are sexually mature and ready to breed within six months.

Harlequin Rasbora

Scientific Name: *Trigonostigma heteromorpha (*formerly *Rasbora heteromorpha*)

Breeding Method: Plant spawner.

Ease of Breeding: Difficult.

Introduction: These colorful little Asian natives make an attractive addition to the community aquarium, but can be difficult to spawn, possibly because they require extreme water conditions.

Sex Differences: The fins of males are redder, as is the rear half of their body. Females are plumper and deeper-chested when they are in spawning condition.

Water Conditions: Very soft and acidic, with a dH of 1 to 3 and a pH of no higher than 6.0, with 5.0 to 5.5 being even better. Some breeders report success using rainwater filtered through peat. Temperature should be between 80° and 82°F.

Equipment: A tank of at least 10 gallons, with subdued lighting and a bare bottom. Add pots of broad-leaved plants such as those of the genera *Alternanthera, Cryptocoryne, Echinodorus,* and *Microsorum.*

Conditioning and Triggers: Condition males and females separately by feeding live, frozen, and freeze-dried food. When female is plump with eggs, transfer the two to a breeding tank and leave them alone to adjust.

Spawning: Within a week, the male should begin flaring his fins and cavorting in front of the female; then the two will cruise the tank together. When they find a suitable leaf on which to spawn, they turn upside down and he wraps his tail over her body, helping her to synchronize the release of her eggs with that of his milt. The fertilized eggs, which are roughly the size of a pinhead but hard to see because they are transparent, are usually deposited on the underside of the leaf. The pair then swims around together some more, chooses another spawning site, and lays more eggs. (Subsequent spawning sites are usually near the first.) When spawning is completed, the breeding pair should be removed immediately, or they will hunt down and eat their eggs.

Brood Size: Up to 200 (younger females often have fewer eggs).

Fry Care: The fry will hatch in two to three days, and become free swimming four days after that. When this occurs, add a mature sponge filter to the tank and begin feeding small but frequent amounts of infusoria and liquid fry food. When they are a few days old, they will be big enough to eat hatched brine shrimp. Do not change water for the first two weeks to a month; after that, change about 10 percent of the water per week, being careful to use water of the same hardness, pH, and temperature. When the fry are about two months old, you can harden the water slightly.

Special Notes: The optimal breeding age for Harlequin Rasboras seems to be seven or eight months. By the time they are 20 months old, most females will no longer spawn.

Species with Similar Breeding Habits: Pygmy Rasbora (Rasbora maculata).

Part 2

Scissortail Rasbora

Scientific Name: Rasbora trilineatus

Breeding Method: Egg scatterer.

Ease of Breeding: Difficult, as is rearing the fry.

Introduction: One of the most popular rasboras, this fish gets its common name from its deeply forked tail fins, which open and close in a clipping movement as it swims. Native to Southeast Asia, it is also one of the larger rasboras, with mature fish sometimes reaching 6 inches in length.

Sex Differences: Can be difficult to distinguish. Males tend to be smaller and more slender.

Water Conditions: The pH range commonly suggested for breeding scissortail rasboras is between 6.0 and 6.5. But some breeders report that they had to drop the pH much lower, to about 5.0, before their Scissortails would spawn. Hardness should be between 4 and 8 dH, and temperature should be 77° to 82°F, with the upper end of that range being preferable. Depth should be about 8 inches.

Equipment: A long, shallow tank such as a 20-gallon long, with several spawning mops placed around the edge and a couple more placed on the bottom of the tank. A spawning grate placed above the substrate is helpful, although not necessary as long as you will be on hand to remove the egg-eating parents after spawning.

Conditioning and Triggers: Condition together on live foods such as brine shrimp. Some breeders say adding black worms to the conditioning regime seems to have encouraged their Scissortails to spawn.

Spawning: Place the conditioned pair in the breeding tank in the evening. Breeding often takes place first thing in the morning. The pair will swim around the tank together, releasing eggs and sperm in mid-water, often next to a plant or spawning mop. Remove the adults after spawning is completed, to prevent them from eating the eggs.

Brood Size: Up to 1,000, although broods of 150 seem more common.

Fry Care: The eggs will hatch in one to two days. When the fry are free swimming, about three to five days after that, add a mature sponge filter, bubbling gently, and begin feeding baby brine shrimp two or three times a day. (Some breeders recommend against feeding infusoria, because the fry seem unusually sensitive to the microorganisms it contains.) As the fry grow, you can add microworms and vinegar eels to their diet. Wait till they are several weeks old before beginning water changes, and then change only about 10 to 20 percent a week, being careful to match the temperature, pH, and hardness. Because Scissortails produce so many fry, be prepared to split them up into different tanks as they grow.

Rainbowfish

Native to Australia and New Guinea, rainbowfish are sometimes overlooked by aquarists–probably because their juvenile coloration is subdued and their price tag is often high. That's a shame, because rainbowfish are peaceful, hardy, and active–in other words, ideal occupants of community tanks–and their adult colors are nothing short

Rainbowfishes are some of the most spectacularly-colored fishes available to hobbyists.

of stunning. They are egg layers, and most species are relatively easy to breed if given good water conditions. However, raising the fry can be a bit more challenging, since they are very small and sensitive to water conditions.

Boeseman's Rainbowfish

Scientific Name: *Melanotaenia boesemani*

Breeding Method: Plant chooser.

Ease of Breeding: Moderate.

Introduction: These eye-catching fish are one of the most popular rainbowfish in the trade. They grow to about 5 inches in length. Males sometimes get territorial and "posture" with one another, flaring their fins as their colors get dark as ink. However, they rarely injure one another during such standoffs. Boeseman's rainbowfish like to shoal, and while they can be spawned in pairs, they will be happier spawning in small groups.

Sex Differences: Hard to sex as juveniles. When mature, the front half of a male's body is an iridescent gray blue, while the back half is an orangey gold. Females are silvery gray with hints of gold, and their bodies are more elongated than those of males.

Water Conditions: Hardness and pH are not critical, but these fish are sensitive to buildups of metabolic waste in their water, so do regular partial changes. Temperature should be 75° to 79°F. The pH of water can affect the male-female ratio of fry, with alkaline water producing more females and acidic water producing more males.

Equipment: These fish like a lot of swimming room, so give them a spacious tank—a 30-gallon long would be the minimum, but larger is even better. Locate it where it will get some morning sun, and add spawning mops, heater, and a sponge filter. Make sure the tank is covered, as these fish love to jump.

Conditioning and Triggers: Condition a group of three males and two or more females for a week or more on brine shrimp, grindal worms, daphnia, and other live foods. Morning sunlight often seems to trigger spawning.

Spawning: Place the fish into the breeding tank in the evening; courting will likely commence by morning. A male will dance and shimmy in front of his chosen partner, flashing his "courting stripe"—a strip of color that runs from his nose to his dorsal fin—as if it were a neon sign. When the female is receptive, they will dive side by side into a spawning mop, swimming from the bottom to the top as they lay semi-adhesive eggs along its strands. Remove the parents after spawning to prevent them from eating the eggs.

Brood Size: Up to 200.

Fry Care: The egg-laden mops can be left as is, or removed to an otherwise bare rearing tank equipped with a sponge filter. Many breeders recommend picking the eggs off the mop with your fingers and spreading them on the bottom of the rearing tank so they will get the maximum aeration; some recommend adding an airstone for the same reason. The eggs begin to hatch in roughly a week, and fry become free swimming a few days after that. They are extremely tiny and should be fed infusoria, liquid fry food, and/or green water. Add baby brine shrimp as they grow. Wring the sponge filter out regularly in lukewarm water and keep it set to the gentlest of bubbles so fry will not tire from fighting the current. Rainbowfish fry are as sensitive as adults to water quality, so it is important to do small partial water changes every second or third day and not to overstock – a liter of water per fry is about right.

Species with Similar Breeding Habits: Red Irian Rainbow *(Glossolepis incisus)* as well as other species in the genus *Glossolepis;* other species in the genus *Melanotaenia.*

Forktailed Blue Eyes

Scientific Name: *Pseudomugil furcatus*

Breeding Method: Plant chooser.

Ease of Breeding: Moderate.

Introduction: These small silvery fish rainbowfish take their name from their unusual blue eyes and their deeply notched tails. They are hardy and easily adapt to a wide range of water conditions. They are most comfortable in groups of six or more, with a ratio of at least 2:1 females to males.

Sex Differences: Males are more colorful, with brilliant canary-yellow fins that grow more intense when they are in spawning condition. The tip of their dorsal fin extends beyond the base of the second, while that of females does not.

Water Conditions: Hardness and pH not critical, although most breeders aim for medium-hard water with a pH slightly above neutral. Temperature should be 75° to 79°F.

Equipment: A 15 or 20-gallon tank located where it will get some morning sun. Add a heater and sponge filter, as well as Java moss, bushy plants, or spawning mops. Some breeders recommend adding a thin layer of dark gravel to cut reflection on the bottom of the tank; it also provides a potential spawning site, since in nature, these fish are known to occasionally spawn on the substrate.

Conditioning and Triggers: Condition two males and half a dozen females together for at least two weeks on live foods such as brine shrimp and blood worms. Morning sun often triggers spawning.

Spawning: Males will stake out a territory, usually a plant or spawning mop, then display to the females, flaring their fins as their colors intensify. Eventually, a receptive female will approach and they will swim side by side into the mop, releasing eggs and milt. These fish will often spawn on consecutive days, so you may want to leave the adults in the tank and transfer the eggs (with or without the spawning mop) to a rearing tank.

Brood Size: Five to 10 per encounter, but because the fish often spawn on consecutive days, there may ultimately be a much larger yield.

Fry Care: The eggs hatch in two weeks, sometimes longer, and become free swimming a few days after that. Feed infusoria and green water for a few days, then add baby brine shrimp, vinegar eels, and microworms. Fry are sensitive to water quality, so change about 20 percent of the water weekly, and add a sponge filter to the tank when the fry are three to four weeks old. Prevent overstocking by moving some of the fry to other tanks as they grow.

Species with Similar Breeding Habits: Other fish of the genus *Pseudomugil,* including *P. connieae, P. cyanodorsalis, P. gertrudae, P. ivantsoffi,* and *P. mellis.*

Magazines

Tropical Fish Hobbyist Magazine

The Leading Aquarium Magazine
For Over Half a Century
1 T.F.H. Plaza
3rd & Union Avenues
Neptune City, NJ 07753
Telephone: 1-888-859-9034
E-mail: info@tfh.com
www.tfhmagazine.com

Internet

A World of Fish
www.aworldoffish.com

Aquarium Hobbyist
www.aquariumhobbyist.com

Cichlid Forum
www.cichlid-forum.com

Discus Page Holland
www.dph.nl

FINS: The Fish Information Service
http://fins.actwin.com

Fish Geeks
www.fishgeeks.com

Fish Index
www.fishindex.com

MyFishTank.Net
www.myfishtank.net

Piranha Fury
www.piranha-fury.com

Planet Catfish
www.planetcatfish.com

Tropical Resources
www.tropicalresources.net

Water Wolves
http://forums.waterwolves.com

Organizations

American Cichlid Association

Claudia Dickinson, Membership Coordinator
P.O. Box 5078
Montauk, NY 11954
Phone: (631) 668-5125
E-mail: IvyRose@optonline.net
www.cichlid.org

American Killifish Association

Catherine Carney, Secretary
12723 Airport Road
Mt. Vernon, OH 43050
E-mail: schmidtcarney@ecr.net
www.aka.org

American Livebearer Association

Timothy Brady, Membership Chairman
5 Zerbe Street
Cressona, PA 17929-1513
Phone: (570) 385-0573
http://livebearers.org

Canadian Association of Aquarium Clubs

Miecia Burden, Membership Coordinator
142 Stonehenge Pl.
Kitchener, Ontario, Canada
N2N 2M7
Phone: (517) 745-1452
E-mail: mbburden@look.ca
www.caoac.on.ca

Federation of American Aquarium Societies (FAAS)

Secretary: Jane Benes
E-mail: Jbenes01@yahoo.com
www.gcca.net/faas

Federation of British Aquatic Societies (FBAS)

Secretary: Vivienne Pearce
E-mail: Webmaster@fbas.co.uk
www.fbas.co.uk

International Betta Congress

Steve Van Camp, Secretary
923 Wadsworth St.
Syracuse, NY 13208
Phone: (315) 454-4792
E-mail: bettacongress@yahoo.com
www.ibcbettas.com

International Fancy Guppy Association

Rick Grigsby, Secretary
3552 West Lily Garden Lane
South Jordan, Utah 84095
Phone: (801) 694-7425
E-mail: genx632@yahoo.com
www.ifga.org

WEIGHTS & MEASURES

CUSTOMARY U.S. MEASURES AND EQUIVALENTS

METRIC MEASURES AND EQUIVALENTS

LENGTH

1 inch (in)		= 2.54 cm
1 foot (ft)	= 12 in	= .3048 m
1 yard (yd)	= 3 ft	= .9144 m
1 mile (mi)	= 1760 yd	= 1.6093 km
1 nautical mile	= 1.152 mi	= 1.853 km

1 millimeter (mm)		= .0394 in
1 centimeter (cm)	= 10 mm	= .3937 in
1 meter (m)	= 1000 mm	= 1.0936 yd
1 kilometer (km)	= 1000 m	= .6214 mi

AREA

1 square inch (in^2)		= 6.4516 cm^2
1 square foot (ft^2)	= 144 in^2	= .093 m^2
1 square yard (yd^2)	= 9 ft^2	= .8361 m^2
1 acre	= 4840 yd^2	= 4046.86 m^2
1 square mile (mi^2)	= 640 acre	= 2.59 km^2

1 sq centimeter (cm^2)	= 100 mm^2	= .155 in^2
1 sq meter (m^2)	= 10,000 cm^2	= 1.196 yd^2
1 hectare (ha)	= 10,000 m^2	= 2.4711 acres
1 sq kilometer (km^2)	= 100 ha	= .3861 mi^2

WEIGHT

1 ounce (oz)	= 437.5 grains	= 28.35 g
1 pound (lb)	= 16 oz	= .4536 kg
1 short ton	= 2000 lb	= .9072 t
1 long ton	= 2240 lb	= 1.0161 t

1 milligram (mg)		= .0154 grain
1 gram (g)	= 1000 mg	= .0353 oz
1 kilogram (kg)	= 1000 g	= 2.2046 lb
1 tonne (t)	= 1000 kg	= 1.1023 short tons
1 tonne		= .9842 long ton

VOLUME

1 cubic inch (in^3)		= 16.387 cm^3
1 cubic foot (ft^3)	= 1728 in^3	= .028 m^3
1 cubic yard (yd^3)	= 27 ft^3	= .7646 m^3
1 fluid ounce (fl oz)		= 2.957 cl
1 liquid pint (pt)	= 16 fl oz	= .4732 l
1 liquid quart (qt)	= 2 pt	= .946 l
1 gallon (gal)	= 4 qt	= 3.7853 l
1 dry pint		= .5506 l
1 bushel (bu)	= 64 dry pt	= 35.2381 l

1 cubic centimeter (cm^3)		= .061 in^3
1 cubic decimeter (dm^3)	= 1000 cm^3	= .353 ft^3
1 cubic meter (m^3)	= 1000 dm^3	= 1.3079 yd^3
1 liter (l)	= 1 dm^3	= .2642 gal
1 hectoliter (hl)	= 100 l	= 2.8378 bu

TEMPERATURE

C° 25° 18° 10° 0° 10° 20° 30° 40° 50° 60° 70° 80° 90° 100°

F° -13° 0° 10° 20° 32° 40° 50° 60° 70° 80° 90° 100° 110° 120° 130° 140° 150° 160° 170° 180° 190° 200° 212°

CELSIUS° = 5/9 (F° − 32°)   FAHRENHEIT° = 9/5 C° + 32°

Index

Photo Credits